WE NEED TO TALK

Saying What WE Need To Say Without Hurting Each Other

Dr. Leonard N. Smith

ISBN 978-0-9852969-0-2

Gold Medallion Books
Alexandria, Virginia 22310

www.goldmedallionbooks.com

Cover design by Dejan Jovanovic-Koki
Cover and text design by John Reinhardt Book Design

Printed in the United States of America

Contents

Foreword

I'D BETTER PREPARE YOU. I believe in not beating around the bush with the "real deal" when I counsel couples who are struggling with communication issues and conflict. WARNING—neither does Dr. Leonard N. Smith.

I'm known nationally as the "love doctor" who spares no words to get at the complications that exist between the sexes. In any given week, I'm caught up in "he said/she said" issues with couples who tattle on each other like children when they are in trouble. As a relationship therapist, I have found that couples get into trouble communicating mostly because of three dynamics—***how*** they present their concerns, ***when*** they express their thoughts, and ***how*** emotionally disconnected they are from each other.

The latter stands out among the rest. There are many reasons that couples find it difficult to stay connected. Some couples don't have good role models for communicating. Others are distant because they spend more time with their children or at work than they do with each other. Still others never learned the skills and techniques required for sharing their needs and feelings maturely without bringing irreparable harm to the relationship. That's why this book is so important. If a couple commits to reading and practicing the straightforward tips contained in this book, they'll stand a better chance of working out their issues with fewer challenges.

Since the two major problems people seem to face when communicating are perception and interpretation, this guide to understanding effective ways to share sensitive issues will help couples infuse their relationship with much-needed compassion and understanding. Dr. Smith skillfully walks readers through ways to learn, understand, and manage each other's core vulnerabilities so that both parties will have the courage to face and receive each other's feedback when there's disagreement and conflict. This book may not be the answer to all of your issues as a couple, but it will definitely strengthen you in addressing your communications issues.

In my book, *Getting Good Loving*, I suggest using compassionate power to help couples learn the art of empathy. Compassionate power allows individuals to understand each other without judging or criticizing in a harsh way. Being able to do this can be a big test for some people's ego. Passing this exam, however, will allow each person to not function with unrealistic expectations. This is important because expectations are always at the foundation of judgments. Maybe I should say it again—being unrealistic with expectations leads to negative criticisms. Make note of this if you've ignored everything I've said up to now: No relationship will survive if your partner feels more judged than admired.

Through the years, I have had Dr. Smith on as a guest on my weekly radio program to discuss relationship issues. The same insight and thoughtfulness he shares on the show that has aided so many of my callers are now presented on paper. What a practical and powerful book! It's laced with wit and wisdom, real-life challenges and personal experiences, and yet it addresses the hard facts that will help relationships survive the tough times. So I'm going to give you some simple advice—I'm always giving advice to the lovelorn. Follow the suggestions in this book, and you can communicate better and reduce conflict between you and your partner.

Audrey B. Chapman, PhD
Therapist, Author, and Radio Talk Show Host WHUR-96.3 FM and H.U.R. Voices on SiriusXM Channel 141

Introduction

I BET YOU'RE THINKING, "Nooooo! Not another couple's communication book!" Sorry to disappoint you, but yes, this is another one. But I promise you, it is unlike any other couple's communication book you have read before. I know you're thinking that there are too many such books on this topic making you want to ask, "Do we really need another one?" I don't know if you need another one or not, but I can tell you that there certainly are a lot of couples who do.

I may not be aware of your communication history, but I know that if you are reading these words, you are likely in one of the following three stages:

1. Keenly aware of the importance of healthy communication in a relationship and desirous of such communication in your current or future relationship.

2. Somewhat acquainted with the importance of healthy communication in a relationship, but unconvinced that it is essential to a healthy relationship.

3. Experienced with the results of poor communication and don't want it to happen again.

Such practical knowledge is normally acquired in one of two ways—either you have seen the power of effective communication in a healthy relationship or you've felt the pain of poor communication in an unhealthy relationship.

Believe it or not, successful communication is essential to a healthy relationship and what you glean from this book will help you in all of your relationships, whether it's with family, friends, co-workers, or someone you've never met. The slant in this book is toward romantic relationships—an area of life that definitely needs reinforcement—and by improving your communication skills in your romantic relationship, you will effectively improve your communication skills overall.

In this book, I speak directly to you in my own voice with the sole intent of assisting you in your quest to create conversational competency. I want to help you upgrade your capacity to connect and clearly communicate as a couple. To do so, I will have to get personal. Within these pages, you will not only be privy to the knowledge I have gained from my professional studies and experiences as a pastoral counselor and relationship coach, but you also will benefit from some of the lessons I've learned from my own personal relationship experiences.

Please do not think that writing this book is an indication that I am the world's best relationship communicator—honestly, I am not! There were moments while writing this book that I questioned my fitness as a communicator. However, by the time I reached the last chapter, I was convinced that I did not write this material because I was the best communicator in the world. Rather, it is because I am a better communicator than I have been. The lessons I have learned throughout my life coupled with writing this material have made me even better. I hope you enjoy, laugh at, and relate to what will be shared with you in these pages, but most of all I hope that you will benefit from what I've learned.

The following chapters comprise my humble attempt to assist you in doing two things. First, to be empowered to say what you genuinely need to say to someone you care about; and to say it in a manner that will not destroy him or her or your relationship in the process. Second, to assist you in establishing an open environment in which you and your partner can always be honest. If you and your partner can successfully create such a context, then both of you will be able to share your authentic feelings, fears, failures, fantasies, disappointments, pain, protests, thoughts and troubles with acceptance and without fear of retribution or retaliation.

I caution you not to start this journey as if you are on a one-way street. If you are reading this book alone and you are in a relationship, you cannot receive the maximum benefit unless your partner reads it, as well. If you do it without your partner, you may be tempted to hold him or her to a standard of communication with which they are not acquainted. The two of you can only become better if you play by the same rules. So approach this journey together. Pursue it as partners in search of a closer and more expressive relationship. The results can be phenomenal.

Let me pause here to say that all of the names, stories, dialogues and incidents are fictitious, except where I mention my own experiences.

Finally, please understand that it is not my intent for this book to be a compilation of research and analysis, nor is it a systematic guide to successful communication—so do not consider it as such. Instead, think of this as a good start for you to begin to understand a few basic communication principles. All of which could potentially change the way you communicate as a couple—and ultimately communicate with others throughout your life. I use the word "potentially" because while this is a self-help book, it may not provide all the help you need but it can help you to see that you have a need.

So...Congratulations! You have officially taken the first step toward improving communication within your relationship.

Let the journey begin!

We Need to Talk!

Any problem, big or small, within a family, always seems to start with bad communication. Someone isn't listening.

—Emma Thompson

MEN, IMAGINE THIS: You are sitting in front of a brand new 60-inch television, purchased exclusively for today. You, like the rest of sports-loving America, are about to watch your favorite sports team take on their archrival in the most talked about championship game in history. For this game, you have chosen to watch it at home instead of with the boys. You are dressed in your team's gear, surrounded by your favorite comfort foods and beverages. You have made all of the preparation necessary to enjoy this long awaited and highly anticipated day.

The moment you have been waiting for rapidly approaches! When out from the shadow of another room, comes the woman who is the apple of your eye. She has an expression on her face that you have seen before. It is that look you hate so much, which says, "I've been thinking." Suddenly without any warning she commandeers the remote, lowers the volume and looks you in your eyes and spews from her precious lips those painfully paralyzing words that no man wants to hear, "*We need to talk!*"...

Ladies, how about this one: It has been one heck of a quarter at work. You have been working on the most difficult project you have ever experienced in your life. You have overcome unbelievable challenges. The supervisor subjected you to unreasonable expectations, and your co-workers did not pull their share of the workload. For the past three months, you have worked 14- to 18-hours a day, seven days a week. In spite of the challenges, you saw this as a necessary sacrifice to achieve that promotion that you so desperately need to support your family. Finally, the project that has consumed your life, disrupted your family and robbed you of your personal life will be finished today!

To celebrate this monumental achievement, your best friend has planned a girl's night out. You absolutely cannot wait for the evening of festivities to begin. You are all dressed up and ready to go. The only thing left is the final touches on your make-up. When suddenly, your knight in shining armor slowly walks into the bathroom. He looks at you in the mirror as if he could see through you. Then, using a tone that you are unaccustomed to, he says, "Uhhh, I think *We Need to Talk*!"...

WOW!

When these four infamous words are spoken, they generally give birth to an impulse to leave the room immediately! You think to yourself, "Oh no! Run!" Rather than run, most of us resort to other evasion tactics like avoidance, aggression, absurdity or even humor—none of which prevents the talk from happening. Ultimately, it is going to happen at that moment or some moment later! The best you can do is try to maintain a calm disposition and endeavor to make the conversation as easy as you possibly can. Tough talks are tough for a reason, but they are as much a part of romantic relationships as love is.

As a child, my grandmother employed tactics that by today's standards would be considered abusive to discourage the usage of four-letter words. Therefore, every time I heard one, I would open wide both my eyes and mouth to the extent of their full capacity. While simultaneously covering my mouth with one hand, I would utter "Aaaaaaaaaaaawwwwwwwwwwwwww," as an undeniable expression of my disapproval of its usage. The words, "*We need to talk,*" make me feel the same way most of the time. I somehow want to exclaim some verbal and nonverbal expression that would unquestionably convey my disapproval of its usage. They are perhaps one of the worst combinations of four words I have ever heard! These words certainly do invoke a vast array of emotions, but what they do <u>not</u> do is make you want to talk.

"We Need to Talk!"

This sentence is almost always interpreted negatively, and is considered fair warning to brace yourself for something very heavy. Whatever it means, you know it's not good!

What do you feel or think when you hear the penetrating words, "*We need to talk?*"

Some people hear:

You're in trouble.
You're busted.
I've done something wrong.
I can't deal with you anymore!

I'm going to get you!
It's over!
I'm done!
You're done!
We're done!
You're not what I want anymore.
I'm not happy.
I've reached my limit!
I'm dying!
I'm pregnant.
I've got a complaint.
I'm fed up!
I can't take this anymore!

I think it is safe to say that most of us generally hear the same thing, but translate it differently. At the end of the day, our individual translations connote similar if not the same meaning. Most of us hear "something is wrong," when we hear "*We need to talk.*" And that is usually what it means. That's a pretty painful discovery to make about a relationship that you value. It's hard to accept the realization that something you have given yourself—your life, and your all—to is in trouble. But sometimes those dreaded words need to be said; and the conversation most likely needs to take place.

If successful communication were an objective within your romantic relationship, I would strongly urge you to translate these words in a manner in which you have not typically done. This task is both daunting and difficult, but not impossible. From now on, when it comes to this phrase, focus on what your partner is *actually saying* and not so much on *how they are saying it*. Let me spend a moment deciphering the four potential meanings behind the unsettling phrase "*We need to talk.*"

First, when people who genuinely care about you say, "*We need to talk,*" it is because they have something they want to say. Whatever your partner has to say is probably not going to be something that will make you comfortable or glad to be hearing it; nevertheless, interpret it this way, "I have something I feel I need to say to you." Be cognizant of the fact that what they have to say may be about or involve you but what they want to say is typically more about them than it is about you.

Here is an example:

Day 1: JANE: John,[1] I don't know if you noticed, but you left your dinner plate on the coffee table. I went ahead and picked it up and washed it.

JOHN: Thanks, honey!

Day 3: JANE: Honey, this is the third time this week that you've left your dirty dishes in the living room.

JOHN: Oh, sorry, babe. I'll clean them up in a few minutes.

JANE: It's too late; I've already washed them and put them away.

Day 5: JANE: JOHN! Why must you *always* leave your disgusting dirty dinner plate on the darn coffee table!

JOHN: SORRY! Geez! What's the big deal?

Day 7: JANE: John... *We need to talk!*

JOHN: About what?

JANE: About how you are always leaving your dirty dishes for me to clean up! I'm sick of it! You treat me like your maid and I deserve more respect!

[1] Fictional names.

Let's stop the conversation right there and closely examine this situation.

Here is the LNS[2] translation of conversation #1:

By the time Day 7 rolls around, Jane clearly has something she wants to say to John. Unfortunately, instead of saying it around Day 2 (when she still had some tolerance), she waited until Day 7, so by the time she expressed her feelings, she was irate! Instead of a rational conversation, this couple is about to have an argument.

Remember that I told you before that oftentimes when a person says, "*We need to talk*" they are expressing a need to say something, but usually it's more about them than it is about you. That's exactly the case here. John didn't have any issues with having dirty dishes in the living room. *Jane* was very unhappy and felt that John was both disrespecting her and taking her for granted. Jane wants John to know that it's not her job to clean up after him. Jane wanted to talk because she needed John to know that she wasn't going to be disrespected in this way. It's not necessarily a "deal breaker" for these two, but it's something that needed to be said.

From here, John has a choice: he can listen and understand where Jane is coming from and make a concerted effort to be more diligent about his dirty dishes; or he can continue to have the argument week after week. If he chooses the latter, this relationship probably has deeper issues than a differing perspective on dirty dishes.

The second potential meaning behind the phrase "*We need to talk*" is this—it is often a cry for "more." I know this seems rather broad in terms of its scope, but don't think for one moment that the phrase does not have specific application. Most

---

[2] Leonard N. Smith

of the time, the person who says it is the only one that really knows what that "more" is, but generally, "*We need to talk*" means, "I want more!" More consideration, more care, more concern, more kindness, more appreciation, more of your time, more respect, more attention. Sometimes they literally just want to talk more. You name it; your partner wants more of it. The deeper issue here is that one of you is dissatisfied in the relationship and at the end of the day; the one who wants more essentially wants unmet needs to be met!

When your partner tells you, "I need more from you," they are saying that the current status of the relationship is not in alignment with their individual desires. The two of you entered into the relationship with your own set of expectations. If you didn't share them in the beginning, you're bound to find out if you have the same expectations—or if you don't! If you don't, this "*We need to talk*" conversation is a prime opportunity to get on the same page. Take the time to be sure that what your partner wants is something you can give…and be sure your partner can do the same for you!

Third, "*We need to talk*" could mean just that, but be careful because once this line is used, what follows can be interpreted as embarrassing, entrapment, entanglement or a pointless examination. Since it does have a way of capturing a person's attention, the speaker should be cautious, and guard this moment as an opportunity to negotiate a matter, settle a dispute or otherwise voice a concern.

Let's face it—sometimes couples just need to sit down and talk their issues out. There comes a time in all relationships when difficult conversations must take place, and for the record, uncomfortable conversations don't have to be destructive. Difficult conversations can fall into categories like: "I've got something bad to tell you" or "You're not going to like what I'm about to say" or "I've been trying to tell you something, but you are not listening to me." In such cases, "*We need to talk,*" when said or implied means the person has something to say and requires constructive conversation and feedback from you. It means that your full attention is required.

The fourth and final potential meaning is this—when you hear "*We need to talk,*" your partner is quite possibly at a breaking point in the relationship and the conversation that follows that phrase could make or break the relationship. In general, the first time or few times a person says, "*We need to talk,*" it is not the end of the relationship. It is more of a line than anything else and perhaps an overused line. It doesn't necessarily indicate that your partner is ending the relationship with you, but it does signify that the person who said it is serious about a matter that concerns them.

Let's go back to John and Jane for a minute. John has reached a breaking point.

JOHN: Jane...
JANE: Yes dear.
JOHN: We need to talk!
JANE: About what?
JOHN: About us!
JANE: What about us?
JOHN: Our relationship.
JANE: What about it?
JOHN: What do you mean, "What about it?" All we do is argue! I can't seem to do anything right anymore! I'm constantly feeling like the "bad guy" in every situation! I can't take this anymore!

Let's stop the conversation again and closely examine what John is saying.

Here is the LNS translation of this new conversation:

John is saying: "We need to talk about our relationship because I do not like the way things are. We are not on the same page, and I have decided that if we don't make some major changes, this relationship is going to end here.

John had come to a point where he felt a need to have a difficult conversation with Jane about his feelings regarding the relationship. John initiated the dialogue; it was about John's feelings and frustrations; and he needed to say it to Jane. What he had to say was about Jane, but releasing it was about HIS need.

Jane probably did not want to hear it, but in actuality, she really did need to hear it. I am sure any reluctance to hearing it would have been rooted in the reality that no one likes to hear negative things about themselves or their relationship. We all want to think we have perfect performance in our relationships. However, this is just not realistic. As difficult as it was for Jane to hear, she needed to hear John's feelings. If she had refused to listen, both of them would have continued to live in a world of make believe. Always pretending that all was well with their relationship—when clearly that's not the case. These two are at a breaking point, and without proper communication in place—their "breaking point" will soon become their "broken point."

Couples really do need to talk!

In my professional experiences, the primary complaint shared by most couples usually has something to do with their inability to communicate. It's typically phrased something like this:

We can't talk!
She/he doesn't understand me.

She/he doesn't know how to talk to me.
All we do is argue all the time.
I'm not good at talking.
I don't know what to say to him/her.
I can't tell him/her anything.
He/she doesn't listen to me.
We don't know how to talk to each other.

When couples experience frequent failures to communicate, it is usually a sign that there is unresolved conflict. Unresolved conflict most often indicates that at the root of all of their issues there exists a communication challenge stemming from misinterpretations, miscommunication, or lack of communication altogether. No relationship can be or will remain effervescent and resilient without healthy communication. Few relationships have the potential to survive without it.

Wherever there is minimal or no communication in a relationship, there are sure to be countless misinterpretations. While there is nothing new about miscommunication, misinterpretations and no communication, couples need to be aware that it is the stuff that breakups are made of. When a person who cares about another feels their partner cannot or will not hear them out, it often causes anger and resentment. Such feelings are usually a prelude to a breakdown—which is ultimately a giant step toward a breakup.

Both my personal and professional experiences have revealed that the central issue in a couple's communication is often mutual or a singular difficulty in sharing unfulfilled needs. Typically, either a person cannot articulate their need to their own personal satisfaction or they fail to articulate their need to the satisfaction or complete understanding of their partner. At other times, one wants to spare the feelings of the other person and so simply says absolutely nothing at all.

We Need to Talk!

Why in the world would an individual make such a statement? Simply because that is the way they feel. But even more than that, it is what they need to do. There are a few instances when the statement reflects an authentic need for both parties to dialogue; but typically, it's the cry of a partner in the relationship who needs to release a feeling, failure or frustration. Rarely is the announcer of the statement speaking for both parties. In most cases, the declaration should be stated, "I need to talk to you!" Or "I need you to talk to me." But at the end of the day, "*We need to talk,*" is an appeal to communicate and often rooted in an individual's sense of pain, hurt and disappointment.

POINTS TO PONDER

- Saying, "*We need to talk*" to your partner is like putting up a big detour sign in the middle of a highway. It means that your current path is about to turn in a different direction. It may be a slight lane change or it could be a major U-turn! Don't use the phrase casually because saying it automatically puts your partner on alert.

- Don't be afraid to have the difficult conversations. It's far better having them than pretending there's nothing wrong. It would be terrible to have what would have been a mere "difficult conversation," turn into the breaking point or the complete breakdown of your relationship.

TWO

What's the Point?

Definiteness of purpose is the starting point of all achievement.

—W. Clement Stone

IN THE 1967 MOVIE CLASSIC *Cool Hand Luke*, a character played by Strother Martin uttered a line that lingers in the memory of every viewer. He had just struck Paul Newman's character with a club. The watching members of the chain gang longed to see their hero rise against the odds, but nothing happened. Luke Jackson remained bent, still, and silent. The night was not his to command. It belonged to another with greater authority. "What we've got here," Captain said, "is failure to communicate."

This statement is common to mankind. At some point in life, all of us have or will utter such words—perhaps, not in the same terms, but in like meaning.

Successful communication is extremely wonderful but when it fails it is extremely painful.

So just what is successful communication? Good question! While few people possess the ability to give you a textbook definition, some people can explain it based upon their personal interpretation. Regardless of whether they can define successful communication or not, most people can tell you when communication is <u>*not*</u> good. For the sake of clear understanding, here is a workable definition for the word communication. The Merriam-Webster Online Dictionary provides what I consider to be a great definition:

> *A process by which information is exchanged between individuals through a common system, of symbols, signs, or behavior; also: exchange of information*[3]

The latter characterization is an excellent summation and crystal clear definition; it's an "exchange of information." Therefore, if the exchange breaks down, it ceases to be communication.

How should communication work?

Communication conveys the thoughts and ideas of the speaker. It bears emotions and it shares mental imagery. Whether written, spoken, or bodily implied, communication is the backbone of successful human relationships—but it can also break the backbone of any relationship.

While communication is one thing, <u>*effective*</u> communication is something else.

Effective communication demands that the communicator think before speaking. This is essential because the accurate transfer of thoughts and viewpoints cannot exist without first organizing your ideas into a coherent format. That format, or structure, is critical for imparting understanding. Without it, a message remains primal in focus and intent rendering

[3] Definition of "communication." Merriam-Webster.com. Merriam-Webster, 2012. Web. 10 Feb 2012.

precise understanding impossible. The speaker must organize and transmit words in a manner that enables the hearer to correctly comprehend the exact meaning of the message. Anything less will result in miscommunication.

In the wonderful world of verbal communication, most speakers strive to avoid words that could result in inadvertently offending the hearer. Technically, a speaker who exercises extreme caution when selecting words of communication should be able to avoid every cause for controversy. Indeed, if scrupulous consideration is given to the makeup of the audience, and acute care is given to sentence structure, all possibilities of personal offenses *should* be eliminated.

—Reality check #1: It doesn't always work this way!

If you feel passionately about what you need to say and you spend hours drafting and re-drafting what you want to share with your audience, then undoubtedly, your message will come across crystal clear. How could it not? You have dedicated hours to making sure what you're about to say is perfect. Surely, after all that, there can't be any room for misinterpretation.

—Reality check #2: It doesn't work this way either!

The idea of perfect communication sounds logical, but real world evidence proves it to be faulty at best. Even the most ideal form of communication fails to eliminate every possibility of controversy. Let's face it; it is utterly impossible for you to escape communication failures.

Ask any public speaker and they will confirm that even when they are at their very best, they fail to perform the golden miracle of perfect communication. Someone always misconstrues something that was said. No matter how painstaking the preparation, avoiding the offense of any and all hearers when speaking publicly is utterly impossible. This is not only germane to the public speaker or preacher—it is a challenging reality for everyone striving to communicate.

Unfortunately, what comes out of the mouth is not always a perfect reflection of what is going on in the mind. What is processed in the hearer's mind does not always correspond to the speaker's intent. At its best, communication is imperfect. It is this flawed form of interaction, coupled with faulty interpretation that fractures relationships, ruins friendships, and shatters marriages.

Misinterpreted communication doesn't always mean an error in truth; neither does it indicate that the listener did not agree with what was spoken. In some events, the listener merely objects to the format of the presentation. Perhaps he or she merely disliked certain gestures of body language. Inevitably, a person's perception becomes their reality. A particular motion or gesture can be perceived as an offense that significantly interferes with the listener's reception of a given message. I know it's almost hard to believe, but one simple body movement can cause someone to miss your message entirely. Think about it. How often have you stopped listening when someone was wagging his or her finger in your face? Or how many times have you witnessed your listener shutting down by crossing their arms, putting a hand on their hip, or rolling their eyes while you were speaking to them? Gestures that indicate an air of superiority, pride, or an attitude of disinterest can easily shut down a listener's willingness to receive the message. On the flip side, a lack of gestures or body language or voice inflection can also cause a listener to misinterpret a message. Don't be fooled. Failed communication is not limited to verbal communication.

With the advent of electronic communications, such as e-mails, text messages, and other messaging outlets, failures to communicate have radically multiplied. How many times have you misinterpreted a text message or email? It is relatively easy to do because neither can convey expression or emotions. While I cannot tell you how many times I've misinterpreted the printed or verbal communications of other people, I *can* tell you that others have misinterpreted my attempts at communication just as much and probably more.

This indeed is an enormous problem.

No matter who you are or how hard you have tried to be clear when communicating with others, misunderstandings still happen. At times, you have likely echoed the sentiments of Captain and publicly or privately declared, "What we›ve got here is failure to communicate."

So what's the point of trying to communicate at all? That's a good question! The point is that you're trying to achieve two objectives:

1. To clearly and accurately convey your unambiguous thoughts; and

2. To command the attentiveness of the hearer so that they will listen and understand your message

It's that simple! Well, maybe not. It *could* be that simple, but only if both the speaker and the hearer understand and accept these terms as the goal of communication. For the record, successful communication only occurs when both the one speaking and the one listening acknowledge the same definition of words, terms, and sentences. Otherwise, you still have a failure to communicate.

When two people meet at the same point of departure, mutually agree on the destination, and simultaneously travel the same road, they will typically end up at the same place. However, if either person deviates from the purposed course of travel, the possibility of arriving at the same destination simultaneously significantly decreases. Such failures in focus and direction can potentially ruin a relationship. Repeated failures usually do.

Communication is no different.

Communication is a MUTUAL effort on the part of both parties: the conveyor and the hearer. The process of effective communication demands a tremendous amount of mutual work. Dialogue that is laced with errors in transmission will be plagued with gross misinterpretations in reception. This rarely produces successful communication. In fact, it produces the opposite effect. Dialogue that is laced with errors in transmission almost always produces confusion, conflicts and communication collapse.

We can't deny that there are many legitimate barriers to successful communication; neither can we ignore them. They can and will interfere with the most proficient communicator and foster failures to communicate.

The obstacles can include an individual's:

- Educational level
- Background
- Religious beliefs and customs
- Morals and ethics
- Culture
- Attitude and outlook

At face value, each of these items seems benign and harmless, but in reality any one of them can undermine successful communication. They readily can become very real impediments that often serve as the root cause of major distortions, misinterpretations and failures to communicate. Reconciling your differences on each of these items can turn your obstacles into opportunities for better understanding.

I sincerely hope that you perceive how significant understanding the goal of communication is to a healthy relationship and especially when speaking to your partner about a difficult matter. It is equally critical to understand the goal of your conversation; otherwise you will be wasting words. Superfluous chatter and extra words will only further contribute to failures to communicate.

Long before you speak, you must ask yourself three critical questions.

1. Do I really need to have this discussion?

2. Exactly what do I hope to accomplish through this conversation?

3. What good can come from having this dialogue?

If this is done beforehand, you may discover that the exchange is really unnecessary. Pointless dialogues are seldom productive and usually are not beneficial to your relationship.

Let me take you back to *Cool Hand Luke*. In the movie, right after Captain said, "What we've got here is failure to communicate," he also gave a powerful footnote that was eclipsed by the previous statement. He stated, "Some men you just can't reach."

This statement sounds pretty hopeless upon initial interpretation, but upon deeper evaluation, it is a very useful reminder. Don't just focus on what Captain said; take note of what he did ***not*** say. He did not call it an "inability to communicate." Nor did he say, "I just can't reach Luke." While it's true that there are some people with whom you just won't be able to effectively communicate, there are many more who you will be able to reach with extra effort and clear goals.

This suggests to me that even though they had a communication failure, Ol' Cap hadn't given up on the possibility of eventually communicating effectively with Luke.

There is a sharp contrast between a failure and an inability to communicate. Failure suggests it didn't work this time; inability suggests it simply can't be done. If your relationship is plagued by the failure to communicate, be of good courage! When two people understand the goal of communication, the situation may be serious, but that doesn't mean it's hopeless.

POINTS TO PONDER

- Talking to your partner doesn't mean the two of you are communicating effectively. Keep the objectives of effective communication in mind. Your goal should never be to win—your goal should be to understand and be understood. This usually means you need to do more listening than talking! You were created with two ears and one mouth because you should listen twice as much as you talk!

- Always remember to think before you speak! Too often we blurt out the first thing on our minds, which is typically not a well formed thought or idea. Take time to think about what you want to say and how you want to say it—take note of your tone and body language as well. Once you have that figured out, then and only then should you attempt to communicate with your partner.

- These few extra steps could save you days, weeks, or even years of frustration! And pain! And misunderstandings! And heartaches! And headaches! And divorce(s)! *And*...

THREE

We're Free to Speak

Tis better to be silent and be thought a fool, than to speak and remove all doubt.

—Abraham Lincoln

I REJOICE OVER THE HONOR of being a citizen of the United States of America. Few countries in this world afford ordinary people the inalienable liberties so often taken as an entitlement by residents of this nation. By virtue of the First Amendment of our Constitution, Americans rightfully enjoy the freedom to live out religious beliefs, participate in public assemblies, petition the Government for deep-seated changes, and aggressively practice freedom of the press.

As much as I appreciate and employ the liberties within this nation, I am convinced that neither America, nor any other country, actually embraces "FREE" speech. Before you consider me a threat to your civil liberties, allow me to state my case. If "Freedom of Speech" is the autonomy to speak without censorship, or repercussion, or retribution, or retaliation, then no one possesses it. It is a self-sustained component of communication.

Theoretically and constitutionally, Americans possess the right to "Freedom of Speech," but this is contained within a context of "Freedom of Speech with a limitation." U.S. citizens are free to say whatever they want, but what they say is often subject to restrictions. Free speech is regulated by the Acts and laws, which govern defamation. For example, slander can result in a civil charge or a criminal offense. Slander prohibits citizens from verbally communicating falsehoods that would in any way defame or otherwise cause harm to the character or name of an individual. Therefore, I have "Freedom of Speech," but I still have to watch what I say. It is a freedom with *limitations*.

What a powerful revelation! Even with free speech, we are not free to say whatever we want!

In most cases, it is common for model citizens to define limitations using the legal parameters established by the law. While that is usually sufficient, our speech should probably be governed by a more narrow set of parameters—much more restrictive than even legal regulations. Such clearly defined boundaries are essential because the occasional misuse of our mouth presents an ongoing struggle for every man, woman and child. Guarding our mouth is extremely difficult for some of us and worse for others—but a common problem nonetheless.

Many times, we speak without regard for the feelings of the person to whom we are speaking. We speak without limitations and say, "They are just words," and we disregard the underlying purpose and intent of what has been said. When speaking, never underestimate or attempt to trivialize the power of your words. Words are not just words. They are powerful expressions of a person's individual perspective, and when those words reach another's ears, they can become extremely harmful weapons.

The bottom line is: Our words have power! Words can give life to a dead situation, or words can bring death upon a living situation. Positive conversation can ignite positive emotions with thriving results. Negative conversations can inflict negative feelings with disastrous results! You have the freedom to say what you want to say, but you must watch what you say—and how you say it! You must remember that you have free speech…with *limitations*! In other words, you are free to speak, but you most certainly have to watch what you say!

At some point, I'm sure you've heard some variation of the classic adage, "Sticks and stones may break my bones, but words can never hurt me." Whoever originated that maxim lied! Sticks and stones may break your bones, but words will not only hurt you, they can damage you permanently. My grandmother shared this powerful affirmation with me as a child, and I believe it to this day. Her purpose was to aid me in my quest to cope with the painful cruelty often inflicted by others in my age group. Kids can often say ruthlessly brutal things to each other. They are often relentless in the recitation of their abuses. In their innocence or ignorance, they say whatever comes to mind because they lack sensitivity. Many times what is said can emasculate the self-assurance of a resilient juvenile and devastate the self-esteem of a fragile one. Many children never develop the understanding that they are free to speak, but not without watching what they say. For some children, the lessons of sensitivity of speech when speaking to others were either never taught or never learned. In either case, these insensitive kids grow up to be tactless adults who cultivate romantic relationships that are destined for and sometimes doomed by communication issues.

As ageless as romantic relationships are, our progress in the area of communicating with each other seems to get further and further apart. Even when you know and understand the mechanics of communication there remains a need for help in this area of life.

In romantic relationships, just as in any other relationship, comfortable moments seldom reveal a comprehensive example of the limitations in your ability to communicate. Growth often requires stress and turmoil. Weak links in your ability to communicate seem always to surface during the most difficult moments in your relationship and usually with grievous results. While this is most certainly true, a couple's communication proficiency cannot solely be measured in moments of crisis alone—it must also be evaluated during your normal, everyday dialogue. Every conversation adds details to the all-inclusive illustration of your individual and collective communication skills.

It's a proven fact that men and women communicate differently. If they are to have a healthy exchange of information and ideas, they must develop a method of discussion that bridges the gap between genders. They must breakdown their respective language barriers and adapt to the terminology that is best understood by their mate. Great care and caution must be exercised when speaking to your partner. In addition, there are a few other considerations for conversing with your partner. Seriously! Everything said in your head should not come out of your mouth. Some things actually should never be spoken.

What You Should ***Not*** Say…

Things like:

- It's all your fault!
- You always…
- You never…
- I hate you!

- I don't want you!
- I don't need you!
- My mother/father told me you were...
- You are just like your mother/father
- My ex never (or always) would have...

As a caring communicator in a relationship, you are not merely limited in what you say and what you should not say. You also are limited in when and where you say what is permissible. This is the rule of thumb: Everything you are *able* to say may not be said at "any" time or in "any" place. There certainly is a time and place for everything. Including what we say to our partner.

The Timing

Often we feel that something is a true statement then it can be said anytime. This is far from the truth. Attempting to talk with your partner when they are otherwise preoccupied is by no means suggested. I wouldn't attempt to talk about a matter that is pertinent to my relationship when my partner is watching her favorite television show, working on a project due at work, or studying for an exam. It's counter productive to communicate about something serious when your partner has had a rough day at the office, is preparing for a major event, managing a family crisis, or grieving the loss of a loved one or friend. When someone is emotionally struggling or hurting from another traumatic or life-altering experience, your discussion will surely be unproductive. Such attempts are designed, destined and doomed for failure.

When seeking to have a serious conversation, be sure to <u>set a time</u> when the two of you anticipate there will be no distractions. Choose a time when the two of you are free from other commitments, obligations, cell phones, and you're not angry, tired, sleepy, sick, stressed or emotionally drained. If the matter is that relevant to you, planning a time to talk demonstrates the seriousness of it.

The Place

Sometimes locating a suitable place to talk can be a daunting task. Especially when you have something extremely difficult to talk about. Choosing the right location can make the difference between having a challenging yet civil conversation and starting World War III. I honestly wish I could tell you that a perfect place existed, but there is none. Therefore, you will have to find that place on your own. While I may not be able to tell you where the right place is, I can share a few key considerations:

- Restaurant? An empty restaurant on a Monday night may be a decent place to talk. But a crowded restaurant on a Friday night is NOT the place to talk.
- Home? Home can be a perfect place to talk. Just know it shouldn't be when the kids are awake or when the dog wants to play.
- Park? A park is magnificent!...When you are not surrounded by a lot of people.
- Car? Excellent! ... But only if you find an area that is relatively unpopulated and you're parked!

Just be certain that both of you are comfortable with your surroundings; and be sure that it is a place that is free from distractions.

Posts and Tweets

I need to warn you that you have limits on what you can say electronically. You are not even free to say what you want to say on Facebook and Twitter!

With the advent of social media and networking, it is now possible for us to vent, inform and share information with people whom we know and don't know in a matter of seconds. For many of us, social networking sites are our primary sources for updates on what's going on in the lives of our friends. With the simple click of a status change button on Facebook, we know when an old relationship is terminated and a new one is initiated. No longer do we meet with our friends to share our pain or call them to vent. Thanks to modern technology, on Facebook we can post our problems and on Twitter we can tweet our troubles. Unfortunately, for some people nothing is "unpostable" or "untweetable." (*I made both of those words up!*) For these people, not even the issues we have in our personal relationships fall into these "un" categories. Just like you can't say anything and everything, you cannot post or tweet anything and everything you want either.

Part of the beauty of social media websites, is that they provide a convenient platform to instantly share our feelings, irritation and opinions. Yes, free speech makes this all possible, but with that freedom comes a weighty responsibility. You have the responsibility to differentiate what can and cannot be said or electronically sent.

Some of the things we say are callous, evil and unnecessary. I won't even begin to reference the awful feelings they inflict upon the person that is the subject of such insensitive statements. Regrettably, words spoken or sent electronically can be used as weapons. When using words as weapons, you can potentially damage, destroy or determine a person's views, beliefs, actions, love and relationship. This undergirds the need for freedom of speech with limitations. Exercise extreme caution and extraordinary care to perfect the art of self-censoring for the peace of our partner and the protection of your relationship.

The Audience

Okay, let's be honest... while most of you consider your partner to be your best friend, in addition to your significant other, you have a "BFF" or a "ride or die" friend, that's been with you through thick and thin. This is your friend that was there during your most embarrassing moment, but never told a soul. This is the friend who took her earrings off to fight with you when someone called you something other than your name. This is your "ace" that helped you move, and then helped you move again, and then again.

When you're arguing with your significant other, you often find yourself wanting to explain your perspective to someone else. In most cases, you're seeking validation for your viewpoint and condemnation for your partner's counterpoint. Lucky for you, you can call your friend! Or can you? Over the years, I have learned that what you tell your friend is not soon forgotten. When you're all made up and back on cloud 9 in your relationship, your friend is often still festering about how you were previously wronged. The problem with sharing everything with your friend is that when you've forgiven, your friend hasn't; and if you're not careful, they'll remind you of the pain that your partner caused you in the past.

So where do you turn when you are upset and want to vent? You turn to your partner, and you have one of those "difficult conversations." It's not easy, but the benefit of making sure your argument stays between the two of you far outweighs the burden of having to explain your decisions to someone outside of your relationship. The audience for your argument should only have two seats—one for you and one for your partner.

POINTS TO PONDER

- If you and your partner need to talk, be sure to choose a time when your partner can give you his/her full attention. The last thing you want is to pour your heart out while your partner's mind is on the game or a night out with the girls. To have a productive conversation, make sure you are both focused on the discussion and have time to devote to a meaningful exchange.

- Remember that once words escape your lips, there's no way to take them back. Once hurtful things have been said, damage is inevitable. The severity of the damage may vary, but when you love someone, you should want to avoid damaging him or her at all costs. Choose your words carefully and don't forget that you have freedom of speech . . . with *limitations*!

FOUR

Keep the Main Thing the Main Thing

The main thing is to keep the main thing the main thing.

—Stephen Covey

ONE EVENING, a gentleman was spending some quality time with his girlfriend at his home. While they were inside, a box was left anonymously on his doorsteps. Upon leaving his residence, the girlfriend noticed the mysterious box. It was a woman's shoebox. It aroused her curiosity, and she could not resist the temptation to look inside. She bent over, picked up the package and cautiously opened it. While peering into the open box, she found a letter and several personal items belonging to her boyfriend.

She immediately reached for the letter and did the unthinkable. She opened the letter, and not only discovered five typewritten (single spaced) pages signed by a woman, but she was displeased by what she read. The writer of the letter was pleading for her boyfriend's attention and was concerned that she had not heard from him. Unfortunately, the letter contained an enormous amount of detail regarding a recent trip he had taken, information that would reveal more than he wanted known. The letter unveiled a mystery surrounding his lack of communication during that same recent trip out of town.

In short, by reading the letter, this man's girlfriend learned that he had been away that weekend with the woman who left the mystery box. She had suspected he had gone away with a woman, but she hadn't been able to confirm it and she didn›t know who the woman was until now. The woman's pain and passion convinced her that deception was the best manner in which to handle this hurtful revelation. She resealed the package and went on her way without saying a word. She made a point not to alter her demeanor—this was business as usual.

The following morning, she didn't give any indications regarding her recent knowledge. All that day her boyfriend made repeated calls to her. He called her throughout the morning and afternoon, but it was strange because he was calling a lot more than usual. Later that evening, instead of coming clean about her new knowledge, she began to interrogate him.

She asked, "Oh yeah! Did you get the box I put inside your door?"

"Oh yes! My sister dropped it off," he replied.

Suddenly her tone changed as her eyebrows raised as she inquired, "Uhhhhh, your sister? Did she also drop off the letter that was in the box?"

The guy displayed an expression of disbelief that could not be misinterpreted by any onlooker. "You opened the box?!" he asked.

Struggling to contain herself for fear of laughing outwardly as she laughed internally, she responded, "I didn't know what it was! I was looking out for you. I was trying to save your life!" Her statement reeked with both humor and sarcasm.

For the man, this was not a laughing matter. Unimpressed by her comedy and irritated by her cynicism, he inquired, "Why did you open my box? It wasn't addressed to you!"

Switching from humor to annoyance, she said, "The box wasn't addressed to anyone, dear. Like I said, I thought it was a bomb or something. I was trying to save your life."

In a calm, but charged tone and in a voice of sincerity he stated, "You knew the box didn't belong to you. You had not right to open it!"

"Like I said, I thought it was a bomb. But guess what?" She confidently asked.

"What?" He passionately replied.

"It IS a bomb because this just blew up in your face!" She said.

At this point, the matter exploded and became a vicious exchange of painful and piercing words. This indeed escalated unnecessarily simply because the couple allowed something other than the main thing to overwhelm the intent of their exchange. What could've been a productive, although difficult, discussion became a dramatic and raw exchange of emotionally defensive responses laced with insults inappropriate to be said by anyone to someone they claim to love.

In this classic case of a couple failing to keep "the main thing the main thing," you will note that the argument was charged with passion as both parties ignored the main thing and sought to win their argument. The goal of communication is not to win, but in this case, as in most, both parties were desperately trying to. Unfortunately, they allowed a new issue to eclipse their intent.

Let's briefly look at the misplaced motives of the two. In the case of the woman, her passion in this dialogue did not come from her desire to resolve the issue. Although it may have started that way in her mind, it ended up with a remarkably different focus by the time the words made their way to her mouth. Why? Two reasons:

First, she did not begin with the truth.

In this instance, as with many, when a person acquires a rumor, gossip, or even factual information about their partner, they want to find out if it is true but seek truth with a lie. So in an effort to protect their sources or method of information acquisition, a lie is born. Think about it. How often have you heard a person say they had a feeling about something when it wasn't just a feeling, they actually had information. Or what if they say they heard something when in reality they just had a feeling about it? Unfortunately, her quest for a confession begins with pretense and pretext—it did not begin with the truth.

When you sincerely love a person and desire to get to the truth, it must be gained by truth. If not, you risk your falsehood becoming the focus and the real issue being overshadowed. One lie does not make another lie the truth; nor are you justified in telling a lie simply because someone else lied to you. If you employ deceit and deception to acquire the truth from a loved one, it will foster distrust on the part of your partner. With each subsequent lie more and more distrust will develop, and before you know it, neither person trusts the other. In case no one has ever told you, trust is the basis of love.

Oh, by the way, a lie is a lie regardless who tells it.

Second, she switched her pursuit.

She knew he would lie, and he did. Therefore, pursuing the lie became more urgent than the real issue for her.

Let me parenthetically mention that I can't understand why people can claim they know a person and yet be surprised by that person's common behavior pattern. If you know what a person is going to do, how and why are you surprised when they do it? It is ludicrous to think a thrifty person will wake up one day and become a lavish spender. It is absurd to expect a pessimistic person to perform like an optimist. So why would you expect a person who lies to tell the truth? Expecting a person to do something other than what you *know* they will do is often called insanity. Setting the scene with incriminating evidence to elicit a certain and predicted response from someone is patently unreasonable, unfair and unrealistic.

This woman's goal to prove he was lying quickly overshadowed the priority of the real issue. The real issue for this couple was not that he was a liar or that he lied, nor was it about the box or what was in the box; it was that the relationship was not mutually exclusive. By not keeping the main thing the main thing, she switched her pursuit and the authentic issue was lost.

Her passion started off as a need to prove to herself that he would do exactly what she expected him to do—LIE! From there, her focus shifted from a desire to validate her own thoughts to an overwhelming desire to prove to *him* that he was lying. Take note of how this entire ordeal is brought to light. She employs pretense and pretext to pursue a confession. By the time the story closes she is lying even more, and the main thing is lost.

Some would suggest that she needed to get all of that off her chest. Perhaps she did, but as I suggested in the previous chapter, *timing is critical!* The timing in this scenario could not have been worse!

Let's look at the man. He did not keep the main thing that main thing for two primary reasons:

First, he wanted to protect himself.

Self-preservation is not just a theory of natural law; it is a normal reaction for most people. Let's take any child. They've been told not to eat any of the fresh homemade cookies recently placed in the jar. You can leave the kitchen and walk back in an hour later and see cookie crumbs around the mouth of the child. Their countenance can be painted with guilt and shame. While that may be true, try asking, "Did you eat any cookies?" and the response will likely be "Noooooooo!" The child knows that there are unwanted consequences for the act of eating the cookies; therefore, the lie is to protect or otherwise preserve him or herself.

This accounts for why the man in the opening story avoids the real issue and attacks his girlfriend for opening the box. He sought to remove the attention from his actions and center it on hers. Keeping the main thing the main thing would have meant he would have had to deal with the mystery woman and his inappropriate actions. Rather than do that, he deals with the box and his feelings of violation.

Sidebar: Honestly, she should not have bothered the box. While it was not addressed to anyone, she knew it was not for her. After all, it wasn't left on *her* doorstep. She probably wouldn't have opened the box if it had been a man's shoebox. Her curiosity does not excuse that fact that this was a violation of her boyfriend's privacy.

Some people seem to think that privacy is forfeited when you enter a romantic relationship. It's strange that most people who feel this way sincerely believe that they tell their partner everything; yet they carry secrets both past and present that they'd never want anyone to know. Why do they keep these secrets from their partner? They fear the consequences and judgment.

Many times self-preservation kicks in before you can even fully process a situation. Pain and fear have a strange way of activating this natural defense. Have you ever told a lie and asked yourself, "Why didn't I just tell the truth?" You didn't tell the truth because you didn't want to suffer the consequences of your actions. The guy in this story is no different.

Second, he wasn't accustomed to telling the truth.

Experts tell us that everybody lies. We all lie and inevitably, it causes problems. While that is true, almost every person you know would agree that lying is dishonest. Telling one lie can be considered a mistake. Telling a second lie would be considered a pattern. Three times or more, you can consider it a problem. This guy obviously had a problem telling the truth. Plain and simple—he is a liar.

Some people lie to avoid trouble. Some lie to protect someone's feelings. Others don't know why they do it. This gentleman did it to avoid trouble, but he had done it so many times before, she was expecting it. So why did he lie? Habit. Why was it a habit? He wanted to look good to himself and to others. So he developed a pattern of lying to preserve his appearance and peoples' perception. This sounds a lot like a self-esteem issue, doesn't it? Well it is!

People who lie in romantic relationships can typically be divided into two categories: Those who desire to preserve or rescue the relationship, and those who lie to conceal mistakes to preserve a perception. Lying may eliminate an immediate problem, but at the same time, it will create an enduring problem.

Here are a few simple steps to assist you in keeping the main thing the main thing: KISS is an acronym for, "keep it short and simple." Herein are two of the very best pieces of advice I can give you to ensure that you keep the main thing the main thing.

First, keep it short!

Make your point and stop talking. The longer you talk about something, the more other things come up. Most of which certainly have nothing to do with the main thing. This is a great defense against beating around the bush and rambling on and on. Brief is better!

Second, keep it simple.

- **Start Properly**: Clearly and confidently say only what you need to say; but be courteous! Sometimes you can think you are being civil, but your tone and body language can say otherwise. Beginning properly increases your chances of ending the way you started.

- **Stick to the Point:** Know what you are going to say and stick to the point. Sometimes you'll be tempted to utter those painful words, *"and another thing!"* DON'T DO IT! Even if your partner brings up something else, get back to the point.

- **Stay in the Present:** Don't deal with what could've happened but didn't; nor what could happen but hasn't. By all means avoid, "the good old days." As well as, "The way things used to be." That was then, but this is now. Stay in the "now" moment.

Keeping the main thing the main thing is often easier said than done. Especially when your attempts to remain on the matter at hand are repetitively derailed by the insertion of insults, judgments, pseudo issues, past events, comparisons to other relationships, or other things that are not germane to the current discussion.

Such insertions can cause the best communicator to become exhausted, frustrated and ultimately angry. This is certainly not the goal of the conversation with your partner nor is it always a deliberate attempt on the part of your partner. Many times it just happens.

To prevent the loss of focus from happening, communicators must faithfully stick with the issue at hand and resist the urge to articulate or vent about something else. Great caution must continuously be exercised to prevent a new issue or insult from eclipsing the purpose of your conversation. Keep the main thing the main thing!

POINTS TO PONDER

- My grandmother used to always say, "Oh what a tangled web we weave, when we aim to deceive!" Those words are still true today. If you and your partner are having a dispute, clearly, you're already in a state of disrepair. That being the case, why make the situation worse by starting an already difficult conversation with a lie? Seeking to catch your partner in a lie by setting up the evidence against them is entrapment and in a court of law, that will get a criminal case dismissed every time! Instead, be honest and up front with your partner, so you can get to the *real* issue at hand.

- Self-preservation is a natural human tendency—but sometimes you have to cut your own throat (and admit your own fault) to get to the heart of an issue. Throwing issues back in the face of your partner to deflect your own shortcomings will only cloud the situation preventing peace and prolonging the problem!

- Every couple argues about lots of little problems—most of which are just that—"little." Those little problems shouldn't be ignored because they are clues telling you that a large problem may be lurking beneath the surface. Don't spend so much time trying to solve the "little" things—instead, get to the root of your issues and keep the main thing the main thing!

FIVE

Own Your Own Stuff!

All blame is a waste of time. No matter how much fault you find with another and regardless of how much you blame [them], in the end, it will not change you. The only thing blame does is keep the focus off you when you are looking for external reasons to explain your unhappiness or frustration. You may succeed in making another feel guilty about something by blaming [them], but you won't succeed in changing whatever it is about you that is making you unhappy. (Emphasis added)

—Wayne Dyer

IT STARTED AS A VERY NORMAL DAY. Harry woke up, said his prayers, did his devotional reading, began planning his day and decided to ask his wife to lunch. She was out already, so he sent her a text asking what her day looked like. She responded and they made plans to have lunch. They met and rode together to a tiny carryout restaurant for their favorite meal. Upon getting their food, they decided to eat in the park, where they spent a couple of wonderful hours together.

After lunch, they went for a ride and concluded their day together at nightfall. Harry was hoping that they could spend more time together, but his wife seemed to be ready to go so he drove her to her car. Although they had a great time, their marriage has been strained for a very long time, and the subtle underlying tension was evident to both of them. They knew the tension was there, but neither wanted to talk about it. They hugged and parted ways.

Once they arrived home, Harry decided he just couldn't take it anymore. Exasperated, he said, "Look! We need to talk! I can't do this anymore!" Harry's wife asked, "What are you talking about?"...

HE: We walk around like everything is all right, but it isn't! I am not happy!

SHE: I've told you time and time and time and time again—I'm not happy either! And you could've fixed this a long time ago, but you didn't!

HE: Oh really? I could've fixed it? Really?

SHE: Yes! Really! You're the one who broke it!

HE: I broke it?

SHE: Yes you did!

HE: How did I manage to do that?

SHE: Because you changed! You are not the man I married!

HE: Well, in case you didn't know it, you are not the woman I married either!

SHE: I don't even know you anymore! Since you got that promotion on your job, I just don't know you.

HE: Like you haven't changed? I can't talk to you anymore. You don't respect me. All you do is gossip with your girls and live like you don't have a husband.

SHE: I guess we're in different places.

HE: I'm sick of you dismissing me!

SHE: I didn't dismiss you! I don't even bother you. I try not to smother you and yet my small efforts aren't appreciated. You give me mixed messages, and I don't know what to do. Accept the fact that I love you and always will, but if you don't love me, or want me anymore, just tell me and I won't bother you.

HE: You definitely haven't smothered me! We hardly ever talk at all. If you want to talk about mixed messages, we could talk about that all day long. But it wouldn't help or change anything.

SHE: I love you!

HE: Yes, you love me, and I love you too, but we can't meet each other's needs. We have no intimacy in this relationship. We don't talk, hold hands, or hug. When was the last time we kissed?

SHE: I don't know.

HE: Exactly! It's been over a year! Love can't exist for long where there is no intimacy!

SHE: I know! But this is the first time you've told me you loved me in a long time. If you told me you loved me before now, things would be different. I never ask for anything. I just want to know you love me. You act like you don't want me.

HE: WHAT? Well what did you think my advances meant? I've asked, more times than I should. Then I stopped asking and withdrew because a man shouldn't have to beg his wife for intimacy.

SHE: Many nights I wanted you to hold me, but you didn't; so I became emotionally unavailable.

HE: Because you acted like you didn't want to be bothered! You were always tired, busy, sick, or it was that time of the month!

SHE: I needed to know I meant more to you than just physical intimacy.

HE: WHAT?

SHE: You don't love me anymore so why would you expect any intimacy! I really didn't think you wanted me.
HE: I NEVER said that to you.
SHE: But you never ask anymore.
HE: Why? So I can be turned down again.
SHE: If you weren't so busy working, maybe you could come home earlier and we could be intimate.
HE: So you're blaming my job for our empty marriage?
SHE: I'm not saying that. But you come home late and I like to go to bed early because I get up before you.
HE: If you were any kind of wife, you'd be meeting your husband's needs.
SHE: It's not my fault. It's all your fault!
HE: That's right, put it on me! I'm not the one who started holding back on you. I can't believe this!

HOLD IT!

In case you are unaware, in romantic relationships difficult conversations will inevitably surface. When they do, it's hard for either party to resist the temptation to take a defensive posture. Subsequently, when one confronts the other, they are typically mentally equipped with their list of ways their partner has contributed to the issue. Once the issue is presented, the newly informed partner quickly seeks to identify the ways the accusing partner is responsible for the issue.

Here's what I mean. During the course of my many years of giving relationship advice and coaching, I've found that most consultations with couples commence in the same way. The visit commences with the first partner expressing that the second partner is either doing something or failing to do something. Then the second partner declares what the first partner is or is not doing, but goes deeper into the impact about the partner's actions or lack of action. They go back and forth; each blaming the other for how they feel. I refer to this as the "Blame Game." Typically this goes on until I get tired of listening to the couple play the game. Many times the issue that brought them to my office is not the problem. The real problem is blame.

This is not abnormal in any way! In fact, blame is rather intuitive and should be expected. The fact that this is instinctive behavior does not mean that it is healthy or productive—it is neither. The goal of blame seems to be to protect an individual's self-image. If any one partner does this long enough, it will spread to the other. Blame is the contagious approach for self-defense!

According to Sigmund Freud, there are numerous defense mechanisms that we unconsciously employ. There may be numerous mechanisms, but I've personally seen two that are more widely used than any of the others. The two are denial and projection. Although you will commonly find them listed separately, the two are very closely related.

Denial occurs when we are confronted with irrefutable facts, and instead of admitting to and accepting them, we reject them and declare them not factual. Denial says, "It didn't happen." It's denying reality or truth. By some standards, this would be considered a lie—and it really is. But our rationale is to deny calling it a lie and instead call it an "act of denial," because it sounds better—more clinical.

Projection is crediting someone else for an act, feeling or thought that belongs to you. It is failing to assume responsibility for your own actions and or issues, and blaming them on your partner. It's rejecting responsibility and relocating it. This is perhaps more common than denial. However, both offer far more severe consequences and pain than confronting your issue.

I am persuaded that one of the ultimate challenges for most couples is refraining from the overwhelming temptation to blame their partner for what goes wrong. It is so much easier to blame your partner; and besides, it feels much better not to be at fault. Just because you don't accept the blame, doesn't mean you aren't the blame. Since men and women have different styles of communication, blaming the other person for your communication issues is easy. This is especially true when you don't understand their thinking and responses; and you believe you are right, and the other person is wrong. This is always where the "Blame Game" originates.

This game is perhaps one of the most paralyzing enemies of couple communication. Many couples never reach agreement or resolution on certain issues because they can't get past whatever that issue is. In actuality, blame is not really a game at all. It is a camouflaged power struggle that prevents healthy relationships from existing.

In order to begin the process of overcoming the "Blame Game," you must alter your thinking and open yourself up to the task of authentically understanding the problem and your role in it. Pointing your finger at your partner never reveals anything about you other than that you are an irresponsible blamer. Remember, as someone once so adequately put it, "When you point your finger at someone, three fingers are pointing back at you."

The Benefits of Ownership

So, why is "owning your own stuff" so vital? Good question! It's really simple! Issues will never be resolved by pretending that they don't exist, or by blaming something or someone else. In order for authentic ownership to take place, it requires you to take full responsibility for all of your actions, reactions and even the moments you have failed to act.

While it is so much easier to blame, taking ownership is incredibly important. Blame may temporarily help you to avoid consequences and pain, but it is never in the best interest of your relationships or for you personally. Ownership is often portrayed as a weakness, but it is indeed a strength. This is critical to understand because many times in relationships, no one wants to take responsibility for their contribution to issues. Such ownership must start with you.

Owning your part is the first step towards resolving the issue. It's hard to do, but if you love someone and you really *want* to work out the issue then you have to be part of the solution. Find the courage to step up and admit where you have fallen short—like Toni Braxton said in her song, *"just be a man (or woman) about it!"* Failing to take full ownership of your role in a situation means that you are essentially admitting that you are not in control of your own life. If you are not in control of your life, someone or something else is. By not taking ownership, you are allowing others to make choices and decisions for you. After all, our lives consist of a myriad of personal choices and decisions. If you blame someone else, you are saying the choice or decision was made for you. How irresponsible can you be?

When you make a poor choice or decision and fail to assume ownership, the *next* time you make a poor decision, you will find that it is even easier to shift the blame. The more you shift the blame, the more you will continue to make poor decisions. The opposite is true if you have the courage to take ownership. I'll be the first one to admit that assuming ownership is not always an easy thing to do. In fact, the level of difficulty increases exponentially when you are in a relationship. However, that is not an excuse not to try. It may be unimaginable, but it is not impossible!

Here's a little known secret. I discovered it in my own personal life. When you own up to your stuff, it can shorten disagreements! Many times, we're so busy trying to defend our actions by blaming our partner that we miss the power of ownership. Try saying, "It's my fault. I shouldn't have done that. I'm sorry." By doing this, sometimes, you defuse disagreements and literally disarm your partner. Caution, in some cases this may make your partner angry. This is because most times if you have a pattern of blame, they will be prepared to combat your defense, but not your ownership. Try it! When you immediately own your own stuff, it not only defuses the situation, it demonstrates your level of growth and maturity too.

Drowning Alone?

Another very subtle way the "Blame Game" gets played is through a twisted tactic I call "The Drowning Alone Syndrome." This occurs when your partner is sharing something with you that you don't necessarily like, or is a bit hard to swallow. After listening to what they have to say, you bring up something about *them* that *you* don't like. As if to suggest, that you did what you did, because of what they did. When in reality, most of the time, one had nothing to do with the other. I call this self-defense tactic the "Drowning Alone Syndrome" because I truly believe that a part and parcel of why people blame is because they are unwilling to drown alone. Let me explain.

As I understand it, one of the worst ways to die is by drowning. It is said to be both a painful and frightening experience, whereby a person suffocates to death in water. A drowning person has absolutely no control over what is happening.

When people are out of control, they will do anything in an effort to sustain their life. That's why you have to be careful when you are near a drowning person. A drowning person will instinctively grab hold of anything or anyone to keep them from going under. They will even struggle and fight to hold on to a nearby swimmer without any regard whatsoever for the life of the other person. As a result, a drowning person can take the other person down with them, as they frantically attempt to cling to life. They do not desire nor intend to cause the death of the other person, but it inadvertently occurs in their effort to stay afloat.

In relationships, when a partner says, "*We need to talk,*" and a painful issue surfaces, the listening partner will perhaps view him/herself as being drowned by the overwhelming issue. Rather than drown alone, they will seek to take their partner down with them. Here's an example:

CINDY[4]: We need to talk about your hanging out late these days!

CARL: What are you talking about?

CINDY: What am I talking about? You know what I'm talking about! You've been coming home after 2 A.M. every night this week.

CARL: There you go! I have not come home after 2 A.M. every night! You always have to inflate everything. I came in two nights after 2 A.M.

CINDY: Well that was two nights too many! Why are you out so late?

CARL: Why do I have to justify why I'm out late? I don't ask you where you've been when you say, "I'm out with the

[4] Fictional names.

girls." What about that? You want me to be accountable, but you aren't accountable!

CINDY: What does that have to do with why you came in after 2 A.M.?

CARL: A lot! I shouldn't have to tell you where I've been if you don't tell me.

CINDY: You don't ask me where I've been!

CARL: My point exactly! So don't ask me!

As you can see, "Drowning Alone Syndrome" is a twisted version of the "Blame Game." While no one wants to drown, we refuse to drown alone. So when we find ourselves drowning, we often take our partner down with us and both of us drown in shallow water.

Reaction Ownership

As I close this chapter, I must broach a side of this matter that must not be ignored. Personal experience has taught me, not all issues in a relationship are shared. In rare cases, the blood and blame is on the hands of one person. Yes, there are atypical instances when you will encounter an issue for which one partner is principally responsible. That partner may assume full responsibility for it or perhaps unfairly share or attempt to pass on the blame. Please understand that in cases such as this, one partner may be solely at fault, but the non-liable partner is responsible for and must take ownership of their *reactions*. This is just as important as the offending partner taking ownership for their behavior.

How you respond to the behavior of your partner, can contribute significantly to the overall problem. In fact, it can cause other problems, some even greater than the main issue itself. Let me give you a few examples, cursing, yelling, ignoring, bringing up old issues, giving the silent treatment, nagging, pacifying, strong-arming, etc., can all intensify an issue. Thereby causing it to escalate beyond reason. It can even be a barrier to full disclosure or a potential resolution to a matter, simply because the non-liable partner responds negatively to the behavior of the other. The couple will cease to deal with the real issue and begin to deal with attitudes. Controlling one's reactions during difficult discussions is essential to effective communications.

POINTS TO PONDER

- **Comprehend.** It's impossible to take responsibility for your actions if you don't understand the problem. This necessitates listening very carefully to what your partner has to say about the issue. Comprehending the problem is the first step to resolving it.

- **Claim.** Take ownership for your part in the issue. Generally, no relationship issue can be blamed solely on one person. For every dime's worth of trouble, each partner paid a nickel. Your role is not to point out your partner's portion of responsibility; it is to claim your own.

- **Change.** Taking ownership for your part in the issue is not enough. What's also required is that you alter your behavior. Many times we want our partner to make all of the changes, and they seem to refuse. I've discovered the best way to motivate someone to change is for you to be the first to change. No one can change you, but you!

SIX

Seeing Through Each Other's Eyes

"You never really understand a person until you consider things from his point of view."
—Harper Lee

THELMA AND THOMAS[5] have been dating for several years. They've had their share of ups and downs and have even overcome some extremely challenging events. They're an average couple, but share an uncommon love. Both are highly opinionated, strong willed and not very open to new perspectives.

On the morning of Thomas' birthday, as a part of his gift, Thelma decides to drive him to work. Upon picking him up, Thomas initially felt a little uncomfortable because he was accustomed to doing all the driving wherever they went; but it was his birthday so he cooperated. Thelma drove cautiously as Thomas looked all around during the rather brief trip. As she drove, he made comments about scores of landmarks

[5] Fictional names.

and sites they passed on the route. Thelma was surprised and puzzled by the remarks that Thomas was making.

Finally she broke her silence and said, "You drive this route almost everyday. You are acting as though you've never traveled this road before." To which Thomas replied, "I've traveled this road before, but never in this seat. I can see things from this seat that I can't see from over in that seat. A different position, gives you a different vantage point."

What a revelation that was for Thomas! He discovered by accident what others (especially Thelma) and even life tried to teach him. An individual's perspective is based on how they inwardly see things outside of themselves. Therefore, it is your perspective that shapes your reality. This means that nothing influences your life and how you see the things in it more than your personal perspective. While there are a number of things that influence your perspective, your position is among the most important factors. Thomas learned that day, that by changing your position, you can change your perspective.

The best cinematic demonstration of this concept, I think, was in a 2008 Columbia Pictures release. Although I am not generally a fan of political movies (partly because I get to witness it in real life almost daily), this one really caught my attention. The film was entitled, *Vantage Point*. It was a dramatic action thriller, which recounted the vantage points of eight people who witnessed an attempted assassination of the U.S. President. No two people told the same story although they all saw the same thing that day. The truth had to be determined from each of the different perspectives. Talk about a mission impossible!

The movie was a great reminder that in every situation, there are multiple points of view. Each is significantly impacted by the position—both physical and mental—of the person at the time. This idea is fundamental in effective communication and must be firmly embraced by every couple that desires to establish and maintain a healthy relationship. Now I'll be the first to admit, most of the time it's fairly easy to forget this principle. Besides, who cares about someone else's perspective? Most of us don't, even though we often say we do. The truth is, if you want a healthy and happy romantic relationship, you'd better learn to care.

In my opinion, the greatest contributor to romantic relationship failures and issues is the inability and out right refusal of a partner to see through the other partner's eyes. While my opening story is a reference to a person's physical position, there are several other positions to consider.

What Shapes Our Perspective?

The answer is rather simple—our perspectives are shaped by the positions we take with regard to several things, including our aspirations, culture, education, experiences, fears, politics, and religion. Let's examine this short list of influences.

Aspirations

Boy do aspirations have a commanding way of affecting your perspective! The things you desire, dream of and hope for can induce you to view things as you *want* them and not as they actually *are*. A great example of this occurs when you first fall in love. You are so enamored that you don't see the other person's imperfections. You see the person as you *want* them to be and not as they really *are*.

Culture

We, who live in the Western hemisphere, live in a pretty self-absorbed society. Therefore, many of us see things based upon an individualist and or materialist point of view. What's in it for me? How will this hurt or help me? How much do I get? From this perspective, we see the world and its opportunities for what we can get out of it and not what we can give. Many of us have sold out to the idea of "It's about me." It's not all your fault that you think that way. At least not according to the experts. The highly regarded University of Chicago Chronicle published an article that speaks to this very idea:

Americans are particularly challenged in their ability to understand someone else's point of view because they are part of a culture that encourages individualism, new research in psychology shows. In contrast, Chinese, who live in a society that encourages a collectivist attitude among its members, are much more adept at determining another person's perspective, according to a new study. "One of the consequences of Americans' problems of seeing things from another person's point of view is faltering communication," said Boaz Keysar, Professor in Psychology and the College. "Many actions and words have multiple meanings. In order to sort out what a person really means, we need to gain some perspective on what he or she might be thinking and, Americans, who don't have that skill very well-developed, probably tend to make more errors in understanding what another person means," Keysar said.[6]

Education

Someone once said, "What you don't know can't hurt you." Not true. The knowledge you lack and the knowledge you possess drastically impacts your perspective. If education is the portal to the world, than the lack of it is a prison of

[6] "Psychological Science," University of Chicago Chronicle, http://chronicle.uchicago.edu/070712/perspectives.shtml

isolation from the world. The acquisition of knowledge will always enlarge your perspective. The more you know, the more you will understand how much you don't know.

Experiences

I would dare say that one's past tops the list in terms of what impacts your perspective. This consists of childhood influences and all of your past experiences. Most often, past experiences form the foundation for your expectations in life. When this occurs, our perspective causes us to see things as we expect them to be and not as they really are. For example, if you grew up always seeing your mother preparing meals and your father taking out the garbage, you might assume that women should always prepare meals while men should take responsibility for outdoor chores. Of course, we know that's not how things always work.

Fears

While fear is a category unto itself, it is also connected to education or having experiential knowledge. The moment you begin to understand something that you fear, you cease to fear it. Here's an example: most people fear snakes. Those of us who fear them typically don't understand them. Most of those who have taken the time to study and understand them do not fear them. If you allow fear to influence your perspective, you will be permanently paralyzed by what you fear in the world.

Politics

The political party you subscribe to definitely shapes your perspective. Whether you are a libertarian on the far left, an ultra-conservative on the far right, or independently independent in the middle—your political stance typically says a lot about your perspective on things.

Religion

The system of religious beliefs you subscribe to most definitely influences your perspective. How you view your God, your fellowman and yourself through the filter of your religion can make you embracing, loving and compassionate or intolerant, judgmental and condemning. I have not seen anything else in the world that possesses the power to push people to extremism like religion. When religion controls your perspective, you see the world as your interpretation of your religious beliefs dictate.

These things and others influence our perspectives and literally cause us to live in our own world. Remember, they shape our reality and our reality is the world in which we live. Of course, we all think and say we see things the way they are; however, that's impossible. We can only see things from our own vantage point or personal perspective. Therefore, we should perhaps say that we see things as "we" are instead of as "they" are. For example, a partner who grew up in a two-parent home will probably see parenting differently from a partner who grew up in a single parent home. The one raised in a two parent home will perhaps be comfortable saying to their child, "Mommy and daddy have to discuss the matter before I give you an answer." Whereas the partner that has been reared in a single-parent home will have no problem saying, "No. I'm not discussing this with your father! I said no and I mean no!" It's not uncommon for a single parent to answer a question without discussing a matter with the other parent and typically, they feel quite justified in doing so. The passion in this answer is rooted in the partner/parent's comfort with their personal perspective.

After living in our own world for a considerable amount of time, it really becomes comfortable, doesn't it? Such a lofty level of comfort makes seeing the world from another person's perspective undesirable. I mean, why would you want to see something through someone else's eyes when it looks so much better through your own?

It's our perspectives that cause us to see things the way we do—almost always one-sided. Many times we fail to see things the same way our partners do simply because we look through different eyes. Rarely is this divide intentional. We're just looking through different lenses!

This reminds me of a joke I heard a joke about two elderly ladies: One day, an elderly lady decided that she would visit her gossip prone friend for the day. The two were indoors enjoying tea, when the woman who owned the house saw her neighbor outside in the backyard. They both noticed that the neighbor was hanging clothes on the line. Suddenly, the woman who owned the house said, "I can't believe that Mary is hanging those dingy white clothes on the clothes line! She knows better than that. How disgusting and embarrassing. She needs to rewash those clothes!" As they both gazed through the window, the lady who was visiting said, "Helen! I think you've made a mistake. Mary's clothes are not dingy; your windows are dirty! If you clean your windows, you could probably see things a lot clearer."

Suffice it to say, dirty eyes will see all things as dirty. The only way to see things clearly is to look through clean eyes. If you see a thing as dirty, you might want to look through the eyes of another person. You'll be amazed by what you might discover.

Tell Me What You See

I imagine that you have seen the picture on the next page or one that's similar before. It's called a visual or optical illusion drawing. Look at is carefully. What do you see?

If you said you see a goblet, you are correct. If you said you see two faces, you are also correct. While what you see and what you perceive in this picture may vary. Neither answer is incorrect. If you only see one, keep looking until you see the other. Here is proof positive that something can be seen more than one-way. If you can accept this principle regarding a picture, then surely you can accept it with regard to how you see things in your relationship.

Wondering why it's important to view things from another perspective even when you are perfectly comfortable with your own? Here's your answer: Because being in relationship demands that you do!

Our failure and resistance to see things through our partner's eyes is primarily because we think we are correct and our partner is in error. The reality is this: if you look from their perspective, you might see that you are the one who's wrong. We're also reluctant to see things from the other person's viewpoint because we fear it may force us to surrender our own. Don't be fooled. You have a right to your perspective, even if it is wrong. Just don't make decisions based upon it without sincerely considering your partner's perspective. In doing so, you will possibly make a decision that is not only bad, it may hurt their feelings as well. I'll admit, many times we make decisions that impact us personally and see no harm in it or potential impact on our partner, only to discover later that our partner was hurt by it and couldn't believe that we would be so inconsiderate. The outcome of such one-sided decisions might open you up to a harsher understanding of your partner's feelings—or perhaps an insensitive tongue lashing that you could have avoided with some forethought. Some, but not all, such incidents can be avoided, if we would just take the time to see our actions through the eyes of our partner before we step out and do it.

A perfect example stems from nothing more than what seems to be a simple miscommunication. Let's go back to Thelma and Thomas. One day, as his workday was coming to a close, some of Thomas' co-workers asked him to go out for a quick bite. Thomas was getting a little hungry, as he always did at quitting time, so he and the crew headed out to dinner. Thomas' decision to go out to dinner was no big deal in his mind. But to Thelma, who was at home putting a dinner-for-two on the table, it was a very big deal. From Thomas' perspective, it was cut and dry. He was hungry, he was asked to go eat, so he went out to eat—plain and simple. He did wonder for a second whether or not he should call Thelma to tell her, but he figured she would enjoy the quiet evening alone. To Thelma, Thomas was being totally inconsiderate by going to eat without even calling to see if she had dinner already prepared. What was inconsequential from Thomas' perspective was a huge slap in the face in Thelma's eyes.

This incident between Thomas and Thelma was a simple example that probably ended in that verbal thrashing I mentioned above. Please note that I said, "*Some* but not all such incidents can be avoided." There is no foolproof method for getting everything right in your relationship or life. Ask me how I know? I wish I had time to tell you! What is right today can be very wrong tomorrow. You are not ever assured that any process, plan or principle will work for you. So never think that anything you try will work the same way every time. You will estimate accurately one day and be wrong on your next try. Today's accurate guesstimate of your partner's perspective may very well be tomorrow's point of contention. You never know what's going to happen. However, failing to try to see your partner's point of view is much worse than trying to do so and being wrong. I know that's difficult to accept, but it is true. I say this because at the end of your scolding for not being considerate of your partner's feelings, you can honestly say, "Honey, I sincerely tried to see it through your eyes before I did it." That always sounds better than, "I didn't think about how you would feel."

Let me close with a couple of notes. First a note to the partner who consistently feels your perspective is being ignored.

Dear Ma'am/ Sir,

STOP IT! Just stop! Stop taking things so personally! No one is sitting around trying to figure out how to hurt you. This by no means negates your feelings, but please remember that your feelings are just that, FEELINGS. Sometimes people (even you, believe it or not) make dumb mistakes, bad choices and regrettable decisions. In some cases, you were probably fondly considered, while in other cases you may have been selfishly left out. While your partner may have a history or pattern of making such errors, there's nothing that says he/she can't learn to be more considerate. Your relationship will have its ups and downs, but at the end of the day, the ups should outweigh the downs.

I encourage you to assist your partner in learning the impeccable decision making skills you have acquired in life. Hold their hand and walk them through it or allow them to learn by trial and error as you most likely did. Applying this notion will perhaps offer your struggling poor decision making partner with some semblance of support as they grow.

Now, here is a note to the partner who repeatedly fails to see through the eyes of their partner.

Dear Ma'am/ Sir,

What is it going to take for you to alter your way of doing things? Yeah, yeah, yeah! I know you selfishly think that you are getting bashed for nothing, but don't you get tired of hearing your partner rant and rave? Look! It is up to you to break the pattern and you need to start today. If you think you have the right partner, you owe it him/ her to make this change. This immature mess is taking a toll on your relationship and eventually you're going to be dumped. People get tired of taking your selfish crap! If by chance you think you have the wrong partner, and you are not willing to try to look at things from their perspective, leave now! Go find the Boo-Boo-the-Fool you desire and deserve!

Your relationship and life can be so much better if you spend some time on the front end of your decisions and look at the impact through the eyes of your partner. You are not a bad person, but you can't keep making bad choices. You should be tired of having regrets. Make the shift today! Your relationship depends on it.

Before I give you a few suggestions to help you to achieve this goal, let me give you my disclaimer.

DISCLAIMER: None of the following steps will work unless both you and your partner are willing to release your own perspective and try to perceive and value your partner's perspective.

Granted, no two people see things the same way all of the time. Plus there is more than one way to look at anything. As a couple, in your communication with each other, you must embrace this principle. Otherwise you will be guilty of ignoring the feelings and needs of your partner.

POINTS TO PONDER

Steps Toward Seeing Through Each Other's Eyes:

- **Admit that it's impossible to always be right.** No matter how much you know (or think you know), you do not know all there is to know about anything. Therefore it is utterly impossible for you to be right *all* of the time.

- **Acknowledge that your partner isn't dumb.** You are not always the sharpest knife in the drawer. Your partner has something to offer. If you think they have nothing to offer, it is more of a reflection on you than it is on them. Why would the brilliant one (you) select someone who isn't?

- **Accept the fact that you and your partner are different, and that's okay.** Do you really want a partner that is just like you? I don't think so. Having a partner that has different gifts, skills and talents is a good thing. They can bring to the table what you lack. It doesn't make you substandard; their presence in your life makes you balanced.

- **Announce audibly your desire to hear your partner's perspective.** Communicate to your partner that you want to hear and understand their perspective. Trust me they have a perspective and opinion. Usually they will give it to you unsolicited or quickly offer it when asked. Your mission, if you chose to accept it, is to ask for it. Once you ask, please be willing to listen attentively. Ask questions and encourage answers, but contain your emotions! Remember this is their perspective and not yours.

- **Appreciate your partner's participation.** Sincerely say and show your appreciation to your partner. Tell them how much you appreciate and value their input. Surely, there will be moments when they may doubt your sincerity, or your appreciation. But remember that it is not about their acceptance of your apology. It's about your authenticity in providing that apology.

SEVEN

We Don't Need to Argue! Or Do We?

"I think both the left and the right should celebrate people who have different opinions, and disagree with them, and argue with them, and differ with them, but don't just try to shut them up."

—Roger Ebert

Marion[7]: Hello Dr. Smith

Me: Well, hello there! How are you?

Marion: I'm okay.

Me: Well it certainly doesn't sound like you're okay.

Marion: I'm okay, but my marriage isn't.

Me: Tell me what you consider to be the main issue or issues.

Marion: I don't know where to begin!

Me: Anywhere you want to.

Marion: I guess the problem is that my partner and I don't love each other anymore.

Me: And how did you come to that conclusion?

[7] Fictional name.

MARION: We constantly argue. It's ridiculous! We can't agree on anything.

ME: Arguing is not necessarily an indication that you don't love each other. Most of the time it indicates that the two of you see things differently.

MARION: You don't understand. We argue every day, and it always escalates. We curse and say mean things—it gets real ugly.

ME: Do you honestly mean the unkind things you say to him?

MARION: I don't, but he means what he says to me!

ME: Wait! Be clear. You can't speak for him. This is about you. Do you genuinely mean the things you say to him?

MARION: (Angrily) Well I said no!

ME: I need you to calm down. I'm not the enemy. I'm here to help, but I need you to give me the same respect that I give to you.

MARION: I apologize.

ME: Apology accepted. Now let's try this thing again. Do you mean the things you say to and about your partner?

MARION: Some things I do mean, but not everything.

ME: What do you argue about?

Marion: Everything! It never stops! We argue over little stuff. It goes on until one of us walks away. We get emotional, and it gets real ugly.

ME: Let's go deeper than the arguing for a moment. Why do you argue with him?

MARION: Huh? I've never actually thought about it. What kind of question is that?

ME: A relevant one, so please answer it.

MARION: I don't quite know why.

ME: Do you ever lose an argument?

MARION: I guess so.

ME: Do you like losing an argument?
MARION: Absolutely not! Who does?
ME: Well say it, Marion! Say, "I argue to win!"
MARION: I argue to win! So what does that have to do with our problems?
ME: It's a sign that you don't understand arguing. Let me share a few things you don't know…

Do couples need to argue? Some experts say we do, and some experts say we don't. All I know is that, like it or not, arguing is very much a part of human relationships. In fact, I am convinced that it is virtually impossible to have a relationship without arguments. I have learned this over time. Regrettably, no one told me when I needed it most.

Growing up, I saw few quality models of marriage. My sainted Grandmother who raised me was a widow twice over; and my mother's marriage didn't last particularly long. Therefore, I depended solely upon the marriages I watched from a distance to be my models. Those that I saw were darned good ones. In almost every case, the ones I admired most were pastors. Of the models I saw, they never seemed to argue. They always demonstrated love toward each other and seemed truly happy. If there was a trace of strain, it was undetectable. They never publicly displayed their personal issues. As a result, I grew to believe that loving couples didn't argue, and if they did, they had to be a mismatch. Therefore, when I got married and argued "all the time," I knew that my marriage had to be all wrong. Nobody ever told me I was the one that was wrong (other than my spouse). If only someone had explained to me what an argument really was, perhaps I would have approached mine differently. Since then I have learned that it takes two people willing to accept their differences to create a partnership. Because they are different, partners will not always see things alike. Shocked? Don't be! It is unquestionably true. Just as I complained that I argued all the time, many stressed couples say the same thing. Perhaps you've said it yourself. You'll always be guilty of saying it unless you fully understand what an argument is.

Here's what I mean:

According to the Dictionary, an argument is defined as:

A reason given in proof or rebuttal; discourse intended to persuade; the act or process of arguing; a coherent series of statements leading from a premise to a conclusion [8]

When you read this definition it is clear that when a couple argues, their argument cannot be characterized by the above definition. Our arguments are not just words being employed to prove our point and persuade our partner. The goal is typically much deeper. Most of the time, couples argue with one goal in mind. It is not to communicate their feelings or ideas—we want to win!

Remember in Chapter Two, I shared with you the goal of communication. However, I did not share with you what the goal of communication was not. The goal is not to win. The goal is to understand and to be understood. This may be surprising, but it is unquestionably true. When people argue, typically they do so with the idea of winning. The goal of winning should never be applied to communication. Normal communication and an argument are quite

[8] Definition of "argument." Merriam-Webster.com. Merriam-Webster, 2012. Web. 10 Feb 2012.

different. Remember, we communicate to exchange information; but we argue to prove and persuade.

During the course of an argument, both parties set out to establish who is right and who is wrong. When winning is the goal, they often resort to excessive approaches to prove their point. Most of the time in the end, neither wins. Usually the participants are even more fixed in their argument and perspective whether right or wrong. The resistance of one normally strengthens the resolution of the other person. Typically, when the argument has concluded, their stubbornness remains. The result is that little to no true communication has occurred. Not to mention that their relationship is left wounded for some undetermined term and sometimes forever. No couple should ever view their difficult dialogues, disagreements and discussions as winnable competitions. This will ultimately prove detrimental to your love and relationship.

If winning isn't the goal of an argument, what should the goal be?

The goal should be to persuade your partner while peacefully raising their awareness to issues, ideas and impacts perhaps not previously considered. If you view an argument from this perspective, and adopt this goal, you will arrive at the conclusion I did. An argument, generally, is not a terrible thing.

However, it often goes sour when the argument turns to anger. Commonly, we view arguments as acts of anger. This happens when we don't understand what an argument is, when we become offended by something said or done, and when we have too many arguments. After all, like anything else, too much of anything is not a good thing. Let's briefly explore anger.

So just what is anger?

Anger is the emotional response that we have to an external or internal event perceived as a threat, a violation or an injustice. [9]

Just like an argument, anger is not a terrible thing either. Well, let me rephrase that! *Controlled* anger is not a bad thing. We all know that when anger is out of control, it is not good! In fact, if you add the letter "D" to anger, you get the word DANGER. Just like anger is one letter away from danger, out of control anger is one step away from danger. Controlled anger is both a natural, extremely normal and even healthy emotion. However, it is a secondary emotion that is normally triggered by a primary emotion. Prior to anger, we initially feel some other intense emotion. These feelings can be one or any combination of the following: attacked, boxed in, disrespected, fearful, forced, hurt, insulted, pressured, slighted, or stressed. Anger is only a visible expression of a concealed primary emotion.

Many times when our partner confronts us with the words, "*We need to talk,*" we feel as though we have just been attacked. They're certainly not attacking us, but it sure feels that way—and no one likes to feel or be attacked. At other times, we don't necessarily feel attacked. Sometimes we feel uneasy when we are confronted with feelings, thoughts or truth. In our state of uneasiness, we reject the reality that is presented to us. Then suddenly we are overtaken by the natural human response of anger and seek to safeguard ourselves.

---

[9] "Understanding Anger." University Health Services Tang Center at UC Berkley. http://uhs.berkeley.edu/facstaff/care/understandinganger.shtml. Web. 10 Feb 2012.

We generally express our anger in one of the following three ways:

- *Aggressively*: By hostilely attacking our partner with the intent to emotionally, physically or psychologically hurt them. Examples: shouting, shoving, slurs, or striking.

ALERT: DO NOT USE PHYSICAL FORCE OR VIOLENCE AGAINST YOUR PARTNER! They don't deserve to be shaken, shoved, scratched, slapped or struck! Physical violence in a relationship isn't something that should ever be taken lightly. If you are in an abusive relationship (physical, emotional, or verbal), you need to get out—and get help immediately!

- *Passively*: We suppress our anger, but later seek to get even. Examples: spreading gossip, silent treatment, ignoring, or destroying property.

- *Assertively*: In this case, we express and address our anger to and with our partner in a nonthreatening manner. Example: Saying to your partner, "I get angry when you…"

Understanding that arguments can sometimes swiftly transform into anger is essential if you ever hope to manage and maximize such moments. Our defensive posture and anger are what lead us to a fight. Although I am not referring to a physical fight, unfortunately they happen too (see my note about what to do when things turn physical), but here I am referring to verbal fights where painful and wounding things are said.

You know the kind of fights I mean—a war of words. The ones where each of you foolishly takes ownership of anything and everything your partner says. You are so centered on the words and behavior of your partner that you never take notice of your own. Back and forth, you each uselessly try to defend yourself against every negative comment the other one makes, only to have your remarks of defense used against you. Each blow begins to weaken you both, but you will not be defeated! You offensively deploy any and every allegation and accusation you can dig up from the past. You defensively employ every threat, negative name and formulate curse word combinations that would make a sailor blush! Whether yelled at the top of your lungs or softly in a cynical tone, nasty verbal fights yield irreversible damage to a relationship.

Though most of the time we don't actually mean what we say, our words leave scars that are difficult to heal. If you desire effective communication and want to provide a safe environment for your partner to say what they need to say without being hurt, you both must view fighting differently.

Friendly Fighting

In order for your romantic relationship to remain healthy, you must adopt a "friendly fighting" attitude. Friendly fighting allows you to use words to disagree without behaving disagreeably. It's saying what you need to say without being intentionally hurtful. Ultimately, the goal is to work things out. To friendly fight is to refuse to allow an issue to become bigger than your love can cover. It's fighting together for what means the most, even when your heart has been broken and your dreams have been deferred. When friendly fighting occurs, often a few days after it is over, you can't remember how it got started chiefly because no wounds were suffered in the process.

Friendly fighters know that whenever there is an issue, it must be dealt with together! They never categorize an issue as "my problem" or "your problem." In a partnership, all problems are community property. Therefore, you should always reference them as "our" problems. Friendly fighters never fight long because they understand that someone has to start the process of reconciliation or there will be no resolution. To them, it doesn't matter who is right or who is wrong, one of the two has to take the high road. They also ask the ultimate probing question of themselves individually, "What am I arguing/fighting about?"

So what <u>are</u> you arguing about?

There comes a point in every romantic relationship, where each friendly fighter must ask himself or herself this meaningful question. This inquiry is less about "What" and more about "Why?" Here's what I mean: When you ask, "What am I arguing about," it plunges you into a serious search for truth. Am I upset about something meaningless or meaningful?

Meaningless clashes are those arguments in which we literally waste our time and energy, while jeopardizing our relationship with marginal matters. Two things will happen with things such as these: your partner will either change his or her behavior or not. Arguing is not likely to change them. If your partner changes their behavior, the matter is concluded; and if they don't change their behavior, you will get used to it. It's senseless and useless to argue over matters that time will take care of.

Meaningless Matters:

- Why hasn't the laundry been dropped off?
- Why did you leave the top off the toothpaste?
- Why did you leave the toilet seat up?

Fights regarding meaningful matters are arguments worth engaging in. This gives credence to the old saying, "Pick your battles." While some things aren't worth arguing over, there are some things that are. In my personal experiences with couples, at the root of most arguments are the following issues: money, quality time, roles and sex. All of these are matters worth arguing about. However, couples don't typically know what the true issue is because they are constantly fighting over meaningless "pseudo" or phantom issues. Most of the time, these arguments are reoccurring because they usually do not get resolved the first time around. This is the normal consequence of centering your attention on things that do not matter.

Meaningful Matters:

- Why did you purchase a new car without consulting me?
- Why do you feel the need to spend more time with your friends than with me?
- Why are you having late night exchanges of electronic communications with the opposite sex?

Sometimes you clash constantly over matters, but can't understand why. It is worth digging into the origin of such behavior. What is the *why*?

What many people don't realize is that their partner does not always do things just to upset them. There are times when underlying issues heavily influence their behavior. For example, perhaps beneath the surface they are haunted by childhood trauma, abuse, and lack of discipline. Sometimes it's ADD/ADHD or other emotional and/or psychological problems. None of these will be remedied by arguing, but all of them can cause serious problems when they remain undetected.

The truth is, arguments will always happen, but how you manage them will determine the outcome. While it is challenging to give guidance on arguing without the benefit of specifics, here are 10 things you need to remember when arguing:

1. Arguing is normal.
2. You are not a wild animal; so don't act like one or treat your partner like one. Keep your anger under control.
3. No one can understand you when you are yelling.
4. You have a choice: You can either run your partner down, or you can run off your anger on a treadmill.
5. Don't attack your partner—attack the issue.
6. No two people will agree on everything all of the time.
7. Compromising is the only thing that can quickly solve your differences.
8. Your partner isn't the only one with a biased perspective; you have one too.
9. You have faults too. Seek to know your own, as well as your partner's.
10. Since arguing is inevitable, be proactive and establish rules for engagement.

Let me close by saying, every argument has two sides. Even if one partner is clearly at fault, the other partner has the responsibility to react and respond accordingly. Going off the deep end will only exacerbate an already unfavorable situation. You don't have to like what your partner has said or done, but if you want to get back to a place of peace, don't make an already bad situation worse by having a reaction that ends up putting you at fault as well.

POINTS TO PONDER

- **Having an argument doesn't mean your relationship is coming to an end.** On the contrary, arguments are normal occurrences. Without them, your relationship would be nothing more than a superficial arrangement between two people. Don't be afraid to argue, but remember to keep it respectful. Don't let your emotions cause you to say things that you will regret once the argument is over.

- **Remember to "pick your battles" and only argue over things worth arguing about.** You shouldn't be arguing without reason—so if you're arguing a lot, take the time to get to the root of the issue. Addressing and solving the underlying issues will help to solve the other petty arguments.

- **Be aware of your mental posture during an argument.** Stop and ask yourself, "Am I being defensive?" or "Am I on the attack?" You may find that you are taking your argument from anger to danger!

- **Physical violence is not an option.** If it happens, take a posture of zero tolerance for it. Quickly seek professional help and alert your local law enforcement authorities. Call 911! Never accept physical abuse as part of your relationship. Not only is it wrong—it's against the law!

EIGHT

We Need to Talk and Not Text

We seem to be preoccupied with the rise of accidental deaths resulting from drivers text messaging. Couples need to be as concerned about the increase of relationship deaths, which can occur when partners text.

—LEONARD N. SMITH

ONE EARLY EVENING I was visiting someone's home that had just lost a loved one. While assisting with funeral arrangements, I could not help but notice that the daughter of the deceased was sitting on the sofa with her head down. I was feeling so sorry for the young woman. Her body nonverbally disclosed her tremendous sense of pain and grief. My heart went out to her. Then suddenly I noticed that she had her smartphone in her hands. Without a warning, she burst into laughter and I was shocked.

I casually asked, "What was that (meaning the laughter) all about?"

She replied, "I'm texting my cousin."

I asked, "Where's your cousin?" thinking that her relative was in some other region.

I was flabbergasted when she replied, "She's right there!"

"Right where," I asked?

Her next statement almost made me fall out of my seat. She sighed, and in an irritated tone said, "Over there!" as she pointed across the room.

I confess my mouth flew open and I am certain I had the look of a deer caught in headlights. That's right! She was texting her cousin who was sitting in the very same room. At that moment I rapidly realized that people don't talk anymore. Not long after this incident, I witnessed personally that many of the people I care about the most would rather text than talk. Since that time, texting is even more prevalent. We have practically stopped talking to each other.

In the December 12, 2010 issue of the USA Today, writer Sharon Jayson affirmed my findings in an article entitled, "2010: The Year Technology Replaced Talking." In the article she asserts:

> *Americans are connected at unprecedented levels—93% now use cellphones or wireless devices; one-third of those are "smartphones" that allow users to browse the Web and check e-mail, among other things. The benefits are obvious: checking messages on the road, staying in touch with friends and family, efficiently using time once spent waiting around.*
>
> *The downside: Often, we're effectively disconnecting from those in the same room.*[10]

The young woman I mentioned above clearly disconnected from everyone in the room, except for the cousin with whom she was exchanging texts. While she may have been electronically "connected" to her cousin, she was not even talking to

[10] "2010: The Year Technology Replaced Talking." USA Today, December 12, 2010.

her cousin or anyone in the room! She preferred to text not talk, and herein lays the major problem.

Teenagers aren't the only ones that have succumbed to the alluring power of technology, so have adults—and if adults do it, than adult couples do it. Computer conscience couples are now communicating and posting their lives and relationships on Facebook, Twitter and other social networking sites via smartphone. Can you believe it? Texting and electronic communications have become so prevalent that we now have text affairs and stalking, "sexting," Facebook romances, and Internet infidelity. Talk about texting replacing interpersonal relationships! Now we are replacing intimacy with texting. It's gotten really bad! Perhaps you don't agree with me that texting has done damage to our interpersonal communications, but you can't deny that it certainly has changed it.

It's changed so much that Christine Morgan wrote the following in an article entitled, *Texting Makes New Couples Jump Into Bed Sooner*:

According to the 1,200 people who took part in the survey by Shape and Men's Fitness magazines, almost four out of five women and three out of five men said they thought texting and using Facebook and other social networks led to couples having sex sooner.

The survey found that the number one method of communication between lovers was text messaging. Women apparently text 150% more than using the phone, with men texting 39% more. It's also a great way to ask someone out, with 65% saying they'd been asked on a date by text and 49% saying they'd been asked out via a Facebook message.[11]

This further validates, we'd rather text then talk.

[11] "Texting Makes New Couples Jump Into Bed Sooner," by Christine Morgan. http://www.mydaily.co.uk/2011/01/27/couples-who-text-have-sex-sooner/

We are constantly watching people make text their primary method of communication. Couples are now using it to express their thoughts, love, affection, hurt, hopes, pain and desires. Can you imagine that? Well imagine this, a couple in the same house texting each other. If you can't imagine that, imagine a wife texting her husband saying, "I'm pregnant," or "We're going to have a boy!" What about text like this: "I want a divorce," "I can't do this anymore," "I'm not in love with you anymore," or "Your mother just died."

As unbelievable as it may sound, couples send texts containing messages just like those. Perhaps you'll agree with me—such messages should be spoken and not sent by text. Yet people do it because they would rather text than talk. That's why, despite all the technology that makes communicating easier than ever, 2010 was declared the "Year We Stopped Talking to One Another."

To suggest that we have stopped talking, by no means infers that verbal output is the only way to communicate with someone. Most of us know all too well that communication is not just verbal. Non-verbal communication can sometimes have a greater impact. I don't know if or when you discovered this reality, but it was made apparent to me as a child. I learned from my Grandmother how influential non-verbal communication could be. She did not have to say anything to me; one look was worth a million words! Depending on the look, I could sense her affirmation or anger with my attitude or activity. Her stare without words could make me chuckle or cause me to cry. She didn't have to talk, but I received the message.

In this postmodern age of technology, in the name of progress, we are watching the demise of non-verbal communication. Technology and the demand for speed and global connectivity have forced us to engage in the new non-verbal communication. It is not a look as in the days of my Grandmother. Rather it is a text. Complete with the massive potential for all of the un-pleasantries associated with miscommunication and misinterpretation. Text messages convey no emotional cues, which leave much to the imagination. Depending upon the receiver's mood, a text message can mean something positive today, while the very same message sent tomorrow can mean something very different.

Because of my own personal experiences, I am convinced that texting is often counter-productive when it comes to the art of couple's communication. When you cannot hear a voice, you cannot fully comprehend the meaning of one's words. The voice reveals emotions. This is why we argue with our partner over the matter of how they say what they say. How many times have you said, "It's not what you say, it's how you say it!" A text leaves so much room for the receiver to misinterpret your message.

Think about how unpretentious statements can come across as rude loud and disrespectful. It really depends upon the reader's mood at the moment.

Here's an example:

Text: "Call me!"

To a person in a pretty good mood, this line can mean, "Give me a call when you can," or "Hey! Call me!" But to the person having a rough day, it sounds more like a demand. More like, "Call me right now! Grrrrrrr!" And PLEASE don't write it in all caps! Now you're yelling! When this happens, a text war is about to begin!

While the debate continues regarding the evolution of mankind, there is no debate when it comes to our technological evolution. With the proliferation of computers, smartphones, emails, social networking and text messages, we have evolved into a society of people who do not talk to each other. I am confident that many would look around at our increased usage of technology and disagree with this idea. They might even go so far as to counter my claim by suggesting, "We've not stopped talking; we simple do it differently." I will agree that we still communicate with each other; however, I maintain the premise that we have stopped *talking.*

Can somebody please tell me what we did before this impersonal method of communicating we call texting? On the one hand, I would warn you against using it completely! But then again, text messaging is not a bad thing itself—only if it is in the wrong hands. Just like a gun is not a bad thing, but a gun in the hands of a bad person is lethal. Some say that text can never replace interpersonal communication, but no one has said it can't hurt it. I fear for the future of relationships with the proliferation of texting. The experts are saying that text messages have become very much a part of dating. So much so that some have said that texts outnumber phone calls among countless couples.

From texting at dinner to posting on Facebook at work or checking e-mail while on a date, I am afraid the electronic communications revolution is quickly becoming the preferred method of communication. Since there are those who are in love with this faceless method of communication, I must insist that you minimize your usage of text messaging. That is if you want to avoid a text fight. That's right! A text fight is inevitable if you, as a couple, make this your primary method of communication. Ask me how I know!

Ever had a day like this one?

You were not upset or angry but you sincerely wanted your partner to know how you felt about something. So what did you do? You quickly snatched up your phone and created a truncated text of your opinion on the matter, and your sentiments surrounding it. Everything was fine until you pushed send! You sat in earnest, awaiting their response. Periodically, you looked at the phone that had not flashed, rung or vibrated since you sent your text. Suddenly a reply comes through. It was not what you were expecting!

Faster than lightening and without any thought—only passion—you fired off a reply. Another one returns even faster than the one you sent. You think to yourself, "WHAT?!" You are now emotionally off center and you cannot believe what you are reading. An innocent expression of your feelings about a matter has now become a text fight!

UNBELIEVABLE! Or is it?

This seems to be the norm rather than the exception for so many couples today. After falling victim to the comfort and convenience of text messaging, the next logical progression is to employ it as a conflict resolution tool. While texting has its positives, there are times when it is the conflict rather than the resolution.

Texting is not a bad thing as such, but it can permanently harm a relationship if you are not careful. Please don't think for one moment that I don't like or utilize technology or actively engage in the practice of communicating via text because I do—every day. However, I have seen the trouble that this form of communication can offer too many times. So maybe I am scarred and scared! I am intentional in trying to keep my texts short, but some of my friends want to hold conversations—they would rather text than talk. What I cannot quite comprehend is how I get myself entangled in these conversations unsuitable for text. All too often text exchanges end up as arguments, misunderstandings and even broken relationships. I'm sure if you've never experienced it, you either don't text or you're in denial.

Unfortunately, assumptions and misinterpretations are routine when texting. Don't get me wrong email isn't much better and for that matter a hand written or typed letter can be bad too. However, with a letter or email if you spend enough time crafting it, you can better express yourself. But with texts, it is almost a no-win situation. I have gotten to the point that I HATE texts! Yes I said it! The "H" word! **I HATE TEXTING!**

Let me give you a couple reasons why I hate text messaging:

1. If you are busy, and you send a brief text, people think you are upset or rude.
2. If your phone dies in the process or you enter an area that has no service, people think that you are ignoring them. And please don't let it happen in the middle of a text fight! They then believe that you have discarded, disrespected, or dumped them.
3. If you don't include a term of endearment, emoticon or other expressive symbol, people might feel unloved, unappreciated or unimportant.
4. If you do it for a long period of time, an argument will start.
5. People will sometimes get offended if you're not in the mood or too busy to go back and forth via text.
6. If you don't respond immediately, it raises questions.
7. I don't view a text apology as a real apology.
8. People have no boundaries and will therefore talk about anything via text. Some things are just meant for face-to-face.

9. People will save text and use them against you.
10. People would rather text than talk!

If you think texting is hard on relationships, try Facebook! I can't tell you how many Facebook wars I have seen.

Text messaging is only effective in sending short few word messages like, "I'll be there soon," "see you at 9pm," or "call me when you can." Other than that, it is not the most effective method of communication. Especially when you are trying to resolve a conflict!

Aaahhh! I got it! Why in the world would someone prefer to text and not talk? I'm glad you asked! Texting is a great mask! You can hide your feelings and conceal yourself from your partner and the confrontation.

In many instances, texting is typically used to preclude face-to-face confrontation and in some instances to prevent emotional intimacy. Texting allows you to confront issues without confronting the person. You can say what you want or need to say without having to experience or contend with the emotions of the other person. Sometimes talking about a difficult matter is uncomfortable, and it would never take place if it weren't for text messaging. I guess you could say that texting is a great confidence booster. Yet it also seems that the people who desire to avoid looking their partner in the eyes or desire to emotionally detach, text so that they can escape hurt, embarrassment, fear or anger.

Please don't misunderstand, texting can and is often used to for fun, flirting, general contact, or to otherwise inform someone that they are being thought of. But when it is employed to engage in challenging conversations rather than brief notes, it's usually much deeper. No matter why you use it, it doesn't replace human interaction. I don't care what anyone else says, a text doesn't and can't replace talking. There is something irreplaceable about human interaction. Sure you can get a dog, but a dog won't replace a human—and a dog won't talk back!

Talking allows you to sort through your feelings and release frustration. It allows you the opportunity to hear another perspective on what's been perceived in your mind. If talking does nothing else, that's enough! Talking is challenging, but in a world where we seem to be obsessed with electronic communication, it adds yet another challenge. How do we confront the challenge of conveying our thoughts and feelings without offense electronically? I don't know! But let me suggest talking because no form of communication can replace the power and intimacy of face-to-face communication. Aside from this method, you are not really engaged in authentic human interaction.

Absolutely nothing can replace the non-verbal expressions that are essential when communicating. No text or emoticon can substitute a smile, smirk or sad expression. What can replace the expressive display that only your body can give? It speaks the truth even when your mouth tells a lie.

Look! If your goal is to have a healthy conversation with your partner, stop texting and start talking. A phone call is better than a text, but nothing is better than face-to-face dialogue.

POINTS TO PONDER

- **Remember the KISS principle!** Keep your texts short and simple...the shorter the better!

- **Never text your pain!** Wisdom does not suggest that you should text your pain. Nothing good can come from it. Resolving conflict via text typically doesn't work and often makes a bad matter worse. Address your issue when you can have a face-to-face dialogue.

- **Beware of addiction**. Don't let anyone fool you! Like anything else, texting can be addictive. And just like any other addiction, you may need help to overcome it.

WARNING: Be careful what you text. People who love you will exclusively share them with friends and save them. But if things go wrong, they just might share them freely and publicly to get revenge. Therefore, the only confidential texts (or emails, pictures, letters) are the ones you never send.

NINE

We Gotta Be Honest

"Integrity is telling myself the truth. And honesty is telling the truth to other people."

—Spencer Johnson

ON DECEMBER 18, 1956, CBS Television premiered a prime time show entitled, *Nothing But the Truth*. By the time, the show aired its second episode the following week; the name was changed to *To Tell the Truth*. This production was aired 1956–68, and remained in continuous syndication until 1981. Since that time, it has resurfaced on several channels, many times.

The show starred a panel of four celebrities that engaged in a challenge to identify a single contestant with an extraordinary vocation or experience. The announcer would describe the real person and then three people would represent themselves as the person described by the announcer. The celebrity panelists were each allotted equal time to question the three. While the "real" person had to tell the truth, the impersonators were allowed to lie in order to convince the celebrities that they were, in fact, the real person. At the end of the questioning period, the panelists voted for whom they believed to be the real person. After the voting was complete, the host asked, "Will the real [name] please stand up?" The real person would then reveal him or herself by standing up.

I loved trying to figure out who the real person was. Sometimes I guessed correctly and at other times I was way off. Whether I was right or wrong didn't matter—I always knew I would find out who the real person was and who wasn't at the end of the game. I was well aware that there was a point where the impersonators had to be revealed. Isn't it a tragedy that life doesn't work that way? Although it is sometimes fun trying to figure people out, unfortunately, you don't always find out exactly who they are. They don't feel they have to be real and many times won't. You can be with a person for years, marry them, live with them and still not actually know them. That's often because the game for them never ends.

To Tell The Truth is no game in real life—it's not for the weak! Most of us demand honesty and swear we give it. Honesty can strengthen your love, or it can destroy it. Honesty is a path to better understanding your partner, but it is also a partition that can prevent them from wanting to know you. It is so powerful, that it can cause someone to fall deeply in love with you; and the lack of it can cause someone to hate you. Honesty is loved, demanded and needed, but all too often it is hated, rejected and avoided. Since the beginning of time, our duplicitous interpretation of honesty has created points of contention in relationships.

Most of the issues faced by couples surrounding honesty stem from the fact that they often don't mutually concur on the definition of honesty. Well, maybe it's not the definition. The definition is clear; but how each person interprets it is not always very clear. Yeah that's it! If two people are not on the same page with regard to what honesty is and entails, they're destined for trouble.

What does honestly mean to you?

Let me ask you a few questions:

Does honesty mean that you tell your partner your every thought? Does it mean you tell them your every mistake? Does it mean you tell them every one of your fears, failures, fantasies, or flings? Does honesty mean you have to tell every dream, disappointment, despair, donation or displeasure? To be honest, must you tell your partner every person you've ever admired, talked to on the phone, eaten a meal with, dated, kissed, touched, allowed to touch you, or slept with?

If it does, then you are not a particularly honest person. Shame on you! Or does it mean that?

If it makes you feel any better, you are not alone. Based on the above, no one is entirely honest. I think I can safely say, in most cases, the interpretation of honesty is discretionary. Just like you get to say whether or not you believe this statement, you also get to determine what honesty is or is not.

Honesty is not always defined and determined by the person doing the confessing. The person that is doing the listening also defines it. It has been my experience both professionally and personally, that most people will label you as dishonest about something that they are guilty of themselves. Let me give you an example: Your partner will be upset with you and call you dishonest because you ate out with someone without informing him or her. Yet, they know they have done the same thing and yet will not call it dishonest nor confess to it.

All of us will publicly confess that being honest is imperative to healthy relationships and declare honesty as one of our uppermost core values. Most people I know will not admit it, but they have a pattern of discretionary honesty too. Just like you! No, I didn't call you a liar! I would never do that! I said you have "a pattern of discretionary honesty." That's not the same as being called a liar. Few ever even notice such a pattern. Usually that's because they're so busy holding others accountable and dispensing judgment for dishonesty. They don't realize they have imposed a standard that they can't even live up to.

Let's be real about this! No one wants to be in a relationship with someone who is a liar. But if you are in a relationship, you are in a relationship with someone who lies. You can tell your partner I said it, and if they say, "I don't lie," run! You just caught them in one of their bigger lies. I'm sure you already know this, so consider it a friendly reminder. Lying is not always what you say; sometimes a lie is what you don't say.

Try this for an example:

Kevin and Keisha[12] are attending a formal gala tonight. Kevin already knows what he's going to wear, but Keisha is undecided. As the time approaches, Keisha puts on a dress that is a little too snug. She knows it's a size or two too small when she asks, but she seeks his approval nonetheless. She turns to Kevin and asks, "How does this look, baby?" And without hesitation or review, he responded, "You look fine honey." Somebody please ring the lie buzzer!

Okay! So is Kevin a liar? I'll give you a clue –YES!

Replay: Keisha asked, "How does <u>this</u> look?" Meaning the dress. Kevin never said anything about the dress. He says, "<u>You</u> look fine honey." Never referencing the too tight dress,

[12] Fictional names.

he opts to answer by saying how she looks. He didn't consider it a lie and you perhaps don't consider it one either. Kevin tactfully avoided the truth; that's a lie by another name—equivocation. If you pointed it out to him, he wouldn't agree. After all, he knows his sweetheart has self-esteem issues, not mention that she thinks she is always right. He doesn't feel like arguing before the event. He knows if he tells the truth, she will get mad. Once she gets mad, she will say, "I don't have anything else to wear. Since you don't like what I have on, you can go by yourself." So to avoid all of the drama, he says, "You look fine honey."

There are times when all of us have been guilty of "sparing someone's feelings." You knew that if you disclosed what you honestly thought or felt you would hurt you partner's feelings. Besides, isn't that what your Grandmother taught you? Mine did. She said, "If you can't say something nice, don't say anything at all." But you know you can't get away with not answering a one-on-one, face-to-face question and look sane. So what do you do? You tactfully avoid the question. You lie!

I'm not trying to paint a completely dismal picture here. Most of the time we do genuinely care about how a person feels or thinks, especially when we tell them the naked truth. We firmly convince ourselves that we are being considerate when we conceal our true feelings about a matter. I guess we subconsciously feel like they can't take our honesty, so we spare them our brutality. As Jack Nicholson so famously said in the movie, *A Few Good Men,* "You can't handle the truth!"

Quick question: Ask yourself, are you really sparing someone else's feelings, or are you trying to spare yourself the drama of that person's *response* to your honesty? Let's just be *honest*—you really aren't trying to spare their feelings. You are trying to avoid looking like the "bad guy" for telling the truth. *True or false?*

An important dimension of effective couples communication is to understand what should and shouldn't be shared. That is a discussion for each couple to have. If you fear having it, do you think that the question will be answered by simply saying, "We share everything?" I think not! People who say they "share everything" with their partner are outright lying. First, because it is impossible to share *everything*. Second, we all know every one of us has secrets. Regardless of how old or small they are; we all have *at least one* secret.

Let me ask you a deep question: Does being in a relationship mean that there should be no secrets between the two of you? Does it mean you have no right to privacy?

According to Dr. David S. Viscott, the answer to both questions is <u>NO</u>. He says:

> *You have the right to privacy—in marriage, in a family, in any relationship, in any group—the right to keep a part of your life secret, no matter how trivial or how important, merely because you want it to be that way. And you have the right to be alone part of each day, each week, and each year, to spend time with yourself.*[13]

Do you subscribe to this theory? If the answer is no, is your "no privacy posture" applicable to you <u>*and*</u> your partner? Or do you decide based upon the issue?

If your answer is yes and you support this theory, what are your privacy limits? Or are there any limits?

I know I'm asking a lot of questions. But they are not for me to answer; they are for your own self-discovery. I just wonder if you know where you truly stand on the issue of

[13] Viscott, David S., "How To Make Winning Your Lifestyle," 1973.

honesty. You and your partner must take time to figure out what honesty means in, to and for your relationship.

"Honesty is the Best Policy." REALLY?

On September 19, 1796, George Washington spoke these words during his Farewell Address:

> *"I hold the maxim no less applicable to public than to private affairs, that honesty is always the best policy."*[14]

Answer this one: Do you agree with George Washington? Is honesty the best policy?

Let's be *honest*! All of us have a story or two that could defend or condemn this idea. We all have an episode (or two), wherein we told the truth and it got us into trouble. Additionally, we can cite an incident where we confessed the truth and were forgiven for the error of our ways. Still the question must be answered, is honesty the best policy? Or does it depend on the circumstance?

Being Honest Has Its Hazards!

I've learned time and time again, when people passionately love you, passion can be disciplined in times of joy; but many times that same passion becomes undisciplined in times of hurt and pain. As a result, the people who will passionately do anything for you when all is well; will passionately do anything to harm you in times of pain. That's right! The very

[14] http://gwpapers.virginia.edu/documents/farewell/transcript.html

people who claim to have unprecedented burning passion for you will throw you under the bus when they are angry. Sometimes the amount of passion they have for you is a sign of the level of passion they will have against you. Therefore, any secrets, rendezvous, confidences, mistakes, confessions are fair game to be exposed.

I am deeply indebted to a very dear friend for sharing this life lesson with me. I shall never forget it. She said, "Passion comes with a price." Wow! Unfortunately, she told me a little too late. By the time she told me; I had already experienced the pain of it. That lesson has been in the forefront of my mind since. Honesty is indeed a two-edge sword.

Okay, can I make a confession? Since I've been cut by that sword so many times, I will tell anyone, sometimes it's hard to be honest.

It is not easy to be honest when you...

1. Know that you'll be punished for your honesty.
2. Know your statements will be twisted.
3. Know you'll be subjected to an extremely lengthy conversation, where you have to listen to the same thing repeated.
4. Know it's going to hurt your partner.
5. Know it is going to anger your partner.
6. Fear that you will inaccurately or inadequately articulate the issue properly.
7. Feel that you can't fix the situation.
8. Fear it will do more harm than good.
9. Know nothing good can come from it.
10. Feel the relationship is over or that being honest will end it.

When I say, "It's hard to be honest," I don't mean it's hard to tell the truth. I am really suggesting that it is extremely hard to be open and transparent on every level. It is painfully difficult to expose your inner most self. Share all of your dreams, passions, weaknesses, pain, regrets, mistakes and failures of the past. To be able to accomplish this monumental task, it requires more than just honesty. It calls for trust. Just like you, I've had my share of people that I thought I could trust, only to discover, everyone who says you can trust them can't be trusted. Sure, in most cases they don't reveal what you trusted them with to the entire world. However, they will tell a friend or a few. Trust me, if a person will tell you their friend's business, he or she will tell your business too.

Still the question yet remains, is honesty really the best policy?

This is such a hot topic! Couples, counselors, coaches and clergy all debate over it and the extent to which it should go. Some suggest that honesty is not the best policy, while others say that it is. What do you think? Or better yet, what do you and your partner think? You will have to answer this for yourselves.

Some advisors advocate that except for planning a surprise party for your partner, you should never lie to them. Well, I don't agree. If a lie is a lie, why would you allow for an "acceptable" lie? This confuses even the liar! This would mean that it is all right to lie under certain predetermined circumstances. What? If a lie is wrong, let all lies be wrong. This is probably why some people think it is okay to lie under certain conditions now.

Let's not get into classifying lies. Next thing you know, people will surmise that all lies are acceptable. Imagine people justifying their lies by saying:

"I didn't lie! I told a celebration lie (about a surprise party)! That's not a *real* lie."

I figure if it is okay to tell a *celebration* lie, then it is permissible to tell a *compassionate* lie (one to prevent hurting someone). If you can tell a *compassionate* lie, it is okay to tell a *convenient* lie (one to get me out of trouble). And if all those are okay, then I guess you can tell people that you don't lie.

Are you confused yet? . . . Yes? Good! My point exactly!

At the end of the day, the two of you need to agree to your own honesty policy. Prior to establishing an honesty policy, you'll first need to agree on what it means to be honest. Then it's on to the policy. Be careful, and do not let your agreed upon policy be a discretionary policy. Don't dare attempt to establish a policy if you have a difficult time communicating, or if there has been a breach of your undisclosed self-designed policy. Discuss the policy when both of you can contribute to the dialogue and collectively construct a fair and feasible policy. You may even need to get professional help with the challenge. In fact, I recommend doing so!

While some advocate, full disclosure, radical honesty, spilling your guts, et cetera, I'm fully convinced that there is something called, "Too much information." You don't have to agree, just continue reading before you judge!

Too Much Information is Often Detrimental

I encourage couples not to dig too deeply into the details of certain matters. It is a proven fact that the deeper you dig, the worse it gets. Nothing good can come out of digging deep into some matters other than more hurt and pain. Which leads to more anger and frustration! Countless times I've seen relationships that could have been salvaged end solely because they dug way too deep. Here, is an example:

Shirley and Brady[15]

The two were in relationship for several years, and planning to be married soon. Brady hadn't popped the question yet, but they were working toward their new life together. One day, a young lady calls Shirley. She says, "*We need to talk.*" Shirley didn't know what she had to tell her, but because she knew her, she agreed to meet with her. Although she didn't know the subject matter, she had a gut feeling that it was about Brady.

They met and soon after their salutations the young woman began to open up. For hours, she dumped facts, dates, times, acts, conversations and events, with added exaggerations on Shirley about a multi-year relationship that she had with Brady. By the time the young woman was done, the relationship and pending marriage of Shirley and Brady were on life support.

Shirley called Brady, and said, "*We need to talk.*" Brady knew what it was about. The other young woman had already informed him that she had told Shirley about their past together; vowing to stop at nothing to ruin his life with Shirley. When Brady arrived at Shirley's house, there was a somber aura about the house. They sat in the kitchen, and Shirley began by saying, "I know everything. So there is no need to lie at this point." She began a series of questions that would make the aggressive Attorney Mitch McDeere, of the television series, *The Firm*. look like an amateur.

She interrogated him for several hours and extracted intricate details. When it came to their intimate encounters, she demanded dates, times, places and acts. You heard me right, *acts*! That is what I call "too much information." She did not need to know the acts that were committed, but her curiosity

[15] Fictional names.

sought satisfaction. And what did Brady do? He told her everything she wanted to know. He genuinely thought by sharing every detail, he would prove his commitment to wanting to work through their issue. Brady had no earthy idea that she would use all of the details to support her decision to end their relationship. There could have been a chance for them to rebuild, but Shirley couldn't accept the acts that he had performed with the young woman.

Someone once said, "The devil is in the details." This is a classic example of that adage.

Let me ask you another question: In your opinion, does honesty mean you have to have *every* detail? If so, what exactly is the benefit? What do you hope to accomplish by hearing it? Sometimes knowing the whole truth can haunt you.

Why do we fear Honesty?

Honesty is not just about revealing a lie, confessing an indiscretion, or disclosing one's past. It also is about not pretending to ignore the little things that eat away at your relationship. These things won't kill you, but they sure as heck irritate you to death. I can't tell you how often I counsel couples on "little things." Something as simple as a wife saying she doesn't mind doing the dishes after cooking dinner—when in reality she thinks it's completely unfair that she should have to cook *and* clean up the kitchen. Or something as mundane as a husband saying he doesn't mind the Friday night "chic flick" dates with his wife—when the truth of the matter is he absolutely hates those movies! What could have been fixed with "Honey, can you help me with the dishes?" or "Honey, can I choose the movie this week?" ends up festering for so long that it eventually explodes into an entirely different issue. What began as an issue over dishes became a wife viewing her husband as selfish; and what started out, as a boring movie night became a husband viewing his wife as a control freak. Is all that really necessary?

Countless couples who seek me out for relationship coaching, often disclose their regrets for not having shared what they felt when things first went wrong. In retrospect, they feel things could have been handled differently if they had only been honest about their feelings from the start. I always ask couples why they didn't feel comfortable sharing their concerns with their partner. The replies vary, but essentially they all sound the same. The answer is fear.

The natural question that comes after this answer is: what kind of fear? Any kind! Take your pick—fear of retaliation; fear of rejection; fear of miscommunication; fear of being alone; fear of hurting each other; and I could list dozens more. Nothing will kill your relationship faster than fear. I encourage you to combat fear together. Fear cannot thrive in certain environments. If you create a loving, open, supportive, non-hostile and judgment-free environment, fear will never be able to terminate your relationship.

Avoid the Deceptive Route To Honesty

Remember the man and woman from chapter four with the late night shoebox drop? Just like that woman, some partners often find out things and covertly solicit a confession from the other by dropping obvious hints. In their minds, they believe that this tactic will inflict enough guilt to force a confession. When it doesn't work, they admit feeling anger and frustration because the hints were ignored or were not apparent to the other partner. This makes the hint-dropping partner feel devalued, disrespected and disregarded. All of which translates into feeling that their relationship is based on a lie.

When your partner employs the hint-dropping method to coerce a confession from you, it might be a good idea to take advantage of the opportunity to come clean. Not that it is the best time to confess; however, given the circumstances, it is your better option at the time. The premium opportunity to confess is the self-imposed occasion—the moment when you decide to share the truth with your partner of your own volition.

When others decide the moment of truth for you, it presents a very awkward situation, which produces unnecessary additional pain and suffering. Coming clean on your own is often vital to the progress and protection of your partnership. It will not only bring you closer; it will aid in the prevention of future honesty issues. Once you confess it, you'll know why it's called "the burden of truth"—it's a heavy load to bear! While it may be a heavy load, it is not as heavy as carrying a lie.

To the partner that would use the hint dropping technique on the person you care about; I say, don't do it! It is wrong! Regardless of how convenient it is or how fulfilling it seems; doing this is not only unfair, it reveals that your partner is not the only deceptive one in the relationship. When you attempt to obtain information using deception, it makes you a liar too. Always remember the saying, "Two wrongs don't make a right." Being up front and honest is your burden too. So don't play games with the truth; be truthful.

POINTS TO PONDER

- **Take the time to establish an honesty policy with your partner.** Don't be afraid to seek professional help in developing it. It's important for you and your partner to have the same definition and interpretation of what it means to be *honest*.

- **There's a thin line between the truth and a lie.** Some would call it quibbling; others would call it equivocation. Leaving out part of the truth or bending the truth is as much a lie as saying that all bananas are blue.

- **No one said being honest was easy.** The burden of truth is called a burden for a reason! Dig deep and evaluate your relationship. If it's important to you, then it's important to choose the harder right instead of the easier wrong. *Be honest!*

TEN

A Case and Cause for Counseling

I've experienced several different healing methodologies over the years—counseling, self-help seminars, and I've read a lot—but none of them will work unless you really want to heal.

—Lindsay Wagner

LINDA AND LARRY[16] have been married for over ten years. They are both attractive, and either can walk in a room, together or separately and command attention. Anytime you see either of them, they possess million dollar smiles, look like they have just stepped out of a fashion magazine and give the appearance of what many would call a "power couple." When they are together, they appear to be quite happy. But if you went home with them, you'd quickly discover that things are not always as they appear. If you observe them very closely, while they appear to be happy in a crowd, to see them alone or at a restaurant reveals a different couple.

[16] Fictional names.

Before the two were married, they had been so in love that they couldn't see their extreme differences. While they looked good together, and both were enamored with the idea of marriage, a key component was missing. Even then, they couldn't really talk to each other. Well maybe it wasn't that they couldn't. It was more like they didn't have very much to say to each other. There was no shortage of small talk, but intellectually, neither received stimulation from the other. Like many couples, they were also significantly challenged when it came to discussing difficult matters, so they did what most couples do—they avoided them. The two somehow really thought things would change after marriage.

Once married, they soon discovered what so many other couples realize after their nuptials. While things do and should change after marriage, not all of them are for the better. As my Grandmother used to say, "You never really know a person until you live with him." This certainly applied to Linda and Larry. Needless to say, their lack of communication did not improve with their new life as a wedded couple—it got worse.

Linda approached me, not as a client, but as a friend. She began to share her feelings, which were less about marriage and more about her husband. I heard the pain and passion in her voice, which was laced with frustration and fear. After listening to her vent for about 30 minutes, I asked her one simple question. "Have you tried to talk with him about what you're feeling?

"Heck no! I can't talk to him!" she angrily replied.

I sensed that I had struck a nerve, so I pursued this uncomfortable subject. I quickly followed up with another question.

"Can he talk to you?" I asked.

"He doesn't even try! He can talk to his friends, but he can't talk to my friends or me. I'm embarrassed to take him with me to work functions because he doesn't know how to talk." She replied.

I heard bells go off in my head, and my light came on! I then asked, "Which one is it? Is it that he *won't* talk to you, or that he *can't* talk, or you *won't allow him* to talk to you?"

She gave me a look that would instill fear in the strongest of persons. I stared back and out of nowhere tears began to run down her face. She broke down for several minutes and wept in silence. Once she gathered her composure, she uttered these words.

"It's not him, it's me. He isn't educated, and I'm embarrassed every time he opens his mouth. He's a good man and works very hard, but he doesn't know how to talk. I hate hearing him destroy the English language."

Now we were getting somewhere. "Linda, have you told him how you feel? I inquired.

She said, "Yes! But he shuts down and then I shut down."

I asked, "How often have you told him this?

"A lot! Maybe too much." She stated.

"Why?" I queried.

"Because he needs to know!" She replied.

I retorted, "So I guess you thought frequently telling him was going to change him?"

Linda sadly said, "I did."

I said, "Well Linda, let me tell you what I feel has happened. Your constant castigating of your husband has caused him to feel like he has been castrated. If he's an average guy, right about now he does not feel that you respect him, because you've attempted to strip him of his manhood."

She interrupted: "That is not what I have done!"

"Look Linda! If you want to save your marriage, it can't be about what you've done. It has to be about what he feels. The two are very different. Talking to me is not going to help this situation. The two of you are going to need to seek professional help with this one." I emphatically replied.

"He won't go!" She said.

To which I inquired, "Have you asked him?"

"No! I know he won't go!" She sadly said.

While this is a page from the lives of Linda and Larry, with a few slight changes it could be a page from the lives of any couple. For many couples, it's obvious that it is difficult, at best, to communicate with each other at times. The average individual will agree that successful communication is essential to a healthy relationship; yet the average couple has communication challenges. Even though, they are aware of the challenges, many will never consider that theirs is a case that warrants professional assistance. Others will wait until it is much too late to seek help.

Not all couples will need a serious regimen of therapeutic counseling sessions. Each case and couple is different. Your situation may require the assistance of a seasoned professional to assist you in your quest to communicate better. There is absolutely nothing wrong with a couple with communications challenges seeking professional help. We often seek professional help with things that we cannot do or otherwise lack the skills to do. You wouldn't try to fix a set of bursting pipes without the help of a professional plumber, would you? Your relationship challenges are no different. Therefore, you should be willing to seek help with communicating just as you would run to call your plumber.

For some reason, there are those who shun the idea of seeking professional help, and go so far as to suggest that it is for people with problems. I think they mean people with problems worse than their own. They feel that if a relationship is not at its worst, counseling is unnecessary. Nothing could be further from the truth. I recommend that you seek counseling the moment you see trouble developing—it's called early prevention. Much like what we do for our physical selves. When we notice a shift in our physical health, we seek the help of a physician before our condition becomes critical.

Like Larry and Linda, most people have communication problems long before they get married, but ignore them. I guess they somehow authentically believe that love will conquer all—communication challenges included. Once they get married and form a team, they soon discover that love really doesn't conquer all. But what they sometimes don't realize is that as with any team, help is essential to winning.

I am thoroughly convinced that one of the primary reasons for the current high divorce rate is the failure of most couples to get a coach for their team. When a professional sports team is not winning, the owner gets a new coach. Couples instead often employ another approach; they get a new player. This is not only true of married couples; it is also true of couples dating.

Many honestly believe that playing musical partners is the solution to their romantic happiness. So they simply repeatedly join the ranks of the "has been" in a relationship or married regiments a time or two—or three, or four, or five, or more. They wake up only to one day discover (if they are honest with themselves), that each time they dumped a partner, they only dumped fifty percent and sometimes less of their communication problem. You can't get rid of your entire communication problem when you are fifty percent of it or more. Come on, let›s face it, you can get rid of your partners, but you are stuck with you.

You can have great players and a bad coach and lose. Or you can have a great coach and horrible players and have a horrible season. A good coach and good players are the perfect combination for a winning team, but not if the team waits too long to acquire a coach. When a couple enlists the services of a seasoned professional, it offers them a haven to share their needs and resolve anger and conflict.

While this is important for us to do—I really hate to admit it—but men (just like Larry) often do not see the need for professional help and many times outright reject the idea of couples counseling. Sorry, ladies, but it's a "man thing." Typically, this is because a part of the natural makeup of a man is to be able to take care of himself, his affairs and his family. Therefore, by nature, he will not ask for help. Much like in the days before navigation systems, a lot of men would rather be lost than to stop and ask for directions.

Men *generally* feel they can handle their own business and do not need anyone else (especially a counselor) meddling in it. Besides, they are not usually open to telling anyone all of their business anyway. Men, this is absolutely the wrong way of thinking! I can't deny that there are some men who are willing to participate in counseling. They typically fall into two classes. First, there are the guys who cynically receive counseling. They don't outright reject it, but they go in thinking that it is a waste of time. Going in with this attitude typically results in them thinking that the sessions were ineffective once they leave.

Second, we have the gentlemen who cooperatively receive counseling. They commendably go with an open mind and a willing desire to improve themselves and their relationships. I cannot overemphasize that when a man like this agrees to seek professional help, it is a very big thing for him. He is saying, "I need help—we need help!" That is really huge!

Now I hope you didn't think that I was implying in any way that every woman wants to go to counseling. If that's what you thought, think again. Take note, throughout this book I used terms like "generally," "often," "sometimes," and "at times." I have deliberately done so because nothing is absolute. I am keenly aware that there are plenty of women who castoff the idea of coaching, counseling and therapy, as well. However, for those audacious ladies who enthusiastically seek it, the experts say they find it effective. Competent, professional help can do so much for a relationship when two people willingly go together. Trust me, I know first hand that you cannot make someone go to counseling; and I also know sometimes you don't want to go either. However, just because you or your partner doesn't want to go doesn't mean you don't need to.

If your communication is failing and you need help, do not delay; your relationship depends upon it. Seeking out the help of a seasoned professional must not be deferred until you're in dire straits! Please don't wait until you *can't* communicate before seeking professional counseling –the sooner the better. Even couples that communicate well can benefit from counseling. Don't get caught up in the stigma that counseling is only for couples that have hit rock bottom. On the contrary, counseling can help you step outside of your own "frame," and allow you to see the whole picture of your relationship for what it really is. You don't have to wait till you hit the bottom! You *should* go to counseling when you first start to feel yourself falling!

Getting help won't hurt your relationship. It can assist a couple in collective growth and promoting a much closer and stronger partnership. However, it can also reveal that a relationship cannot be saved. Unfortunately, it is true that there are some cases when counseling is just a little too late. This occurs when couples allow their issues to fester for much too long. Only to discover they are unable to work through their problems. Discovering that your relationship cannot be salvaged is not necessarily a bad thing! It is far better to come to this conclusion with a seasoned professional, than make such a decision on your own. But keep in mind that no two couples are the same. Each is unique and therefore, has different needs.

You and your partner can save your relationship, but it begins with talking. I know that there are times in most relationships when one doesn't want to talk, and the other doesn't want to listen. This can be both damaging and devastating. When this occurs, you are past the time you need help. Statistics suggest that of the couples that try professional help *before* its too late, most believe it works. While many of the couples that have divorced without seeking counseling live out the rest of their days with regrets, wishing they had at least attempted professional help. Respect the fact that you will undeniably have moments when your issues will become too challenging for the two of you to handle alone. When you need help, don't be afraid or too proud to ask for it!

POINTS TO PONDER

- **Seriously Consider Counseling.** Contrary to popular belief, counseling, coaching, and therapy are not for "crazy" people. It's crazy not to seek help when you need it! You must do it as soon as you recognize that your relationship needs help that is beyond the two of you.

- **Don't Listen to Anybody and Everybody.** When your relationship is experiencing difficulties, family and friends will have a lot to say about it. Typically, their advice is not the very best. They often validate your feelings, but that isn't usually what's best for you. They're too close not to be biased in their opinion.

Seek the advice of a third party professional. I know that cost may be a concern—but don't ask whether or not you can you afford it; rather ask if you or your relationship can afford to go without it.

- **Locate a Nonbiased Seasoned Professional.** A nonbiased counselor or coach is not a person without biases; there is no such thing. It is humanly impossible to be without predispositions. The best you can hope for is a counselor that can bend toward your bias periodically. A truly nonbiased seasoned professional is one that is reputable, doesn't reveal what their biases are, and refrains from being judgmental.

- **Follow up and Follow Through.** Far too often, couples go to the first session or two and stop. They either think that what they received is enough or maybe things get better for a few days and they consider all is well. I liken it to a car accident. If you were injured in an accident, they'd take you to the hospital for urgent treatment. When they discharged you, they would remind you of the importance of following up with your physician or other medical practitioner. Delaying doing so could prove fatal. The same applies for your counseling—so follow up and follow through.